SECRETS OF THE

Southern Belle

SECRETS OF THE

Southern Belle

How *to* Be Nice, Work Hard, Look Pretty,
Have Fun, *and* Never Have *an* Off Moment

PHAEDRA
PARKS

Gallery Books
New York London Toronto Sydney New Delhi

G

Gallery Books
A Division of Simon & Schuster, Inc.
1230 Avenue of the Americas
New York, NY 10020

First Gallery Books hardcover edition November 2013

GALLERY BOOKS and colophon are registered trademarks
of Simon & Schuster, Inc.

For information about special discounts for bulk purchases, please
contact Simon & Schuster Special Sales at 1–866–506–1949 or
business@simonandschuster.com.

The Simon & Schuster Speakers Bureau can bring authors to
your live event. For more information or to book an event contact
the Simon & Schuster Speakers Bureau at 1-866-248-3049 or
visit our website at www.simonspeakers.com.

Designed by Claudia Martinez

Manufactured in the United States of America

10 9 8 7 6 5 4 3 2 1

Library of Congress Cataloging-in-Publication Data
Parks, Phaedra.
   Secrets of the Southern belle : how to be nice, work hard, look pretty,
have fun, and never have an off moment / Phaedra Parks.
      pages cm.
   Includes bibliographical references and index.
1. Charm.   2. Courtesy.   3. Beauty, Personal.   4. Women—
Southern States—Social life and customs.   5. Women—Southern
States—Conduct of life.   6. Women—Life skills guides.   I. Title.
   BJ1610.P27   2013
   646.70082—dc23
   2013013565

ISBN 978–1–4767–1545–2
ISBN 978–1–4767–1547–6 (ebook)

A Southern Belle from her very first breath,
my mother, Regina Bell, raised me to believe
that my potential was limitless.

Mom, I don't know where I would have been without
your prayers and unwavering support.
Your influence and inspiration are evident in every aspect
of my life, and on every page of this book.

° Contents °

° *Introduction* °

Here's what I expect from life: Compliments. Flirtation. Gifts, large and small. Excellent service in stores, and courtesy on the phone. Consideration, admiration, flowers, apologies when appropriate. That's just what a Southern Belle gets from life. Now, tell me—wouldn't you like that, too?

I believe every woman should be a Southern Belle or minimally aspire to being more ladylike, charming, and intelligent, because we should all be treated well. Honestly, I sometimes feel sorry for women of northern persuasion. There they are rushing around in their baggy, drab clothes, doing everything for themselves and looking like they just rolled out of bed. They don't seem to understand there's a better way.

I will say that even in the South, not every woman is a Belle. I can walk down the street and pick them out: this one, not that one, not her, not her. Maybe 20 percent of the women I see are true Southern Belles, and we all recognize one another. It's like being a Mason without the funny handshake. (And I never actually walk down the street; as a Southern Belle, I gently glide in my skyscraper stilettos. But you get the idea.)

The Southern Belles are the women who are completely pulled together. Silver bracelets and gold earrings? Not a Southern Belle. We match metals. But we also have an aura. A halo of confidence, poise, and tranquillity. The Southern Belle knows that she can handle whatever comes her way. No matter how heated the situation, you will never catch a Southern Belle sweating.

It's a commitment, no doubt about it. The Southern Belle doesn't have an off day. My goodness, she doesn't have an off moment. Everybody knows if you have to have a habit, it might as well be a good one. Life is too short for unpleasant or bad behavior. How hard is it to say "please" and "thank you" and remember people's names and keep your roots touched up?

Ultimately, the Southern Belle is about self-respect. She takes care of herself and makes sure people treat her right. Some people might think that this isn't very feminist, but look at it this way: men have to earn respect, right? Back in the day, a lady was respected just because she was a lady. That's all gone. Now we work the same jobs as men. However, the problem is that some men are a little confused about how to treat women. Equality does not equal a man being anything less than a gentleman at all times. I hear that up north, for instance, men don't open doors for women or carry luggage. Well, here's the way it works: I earn a good living, I whoop people's behinds in court, and when I leave the courtroom, I expect someone to carry my briefcase and get that door for me. So I will stand there. I might have to glance around and catch some fellow's eye, but it takes only a moment and let me tell you, the man who grabs that door handle first gets the biggest smile and the warmest thank-you. If he's at all attractive I'll add a compliment on his great sense of taste and style, making him feel like Superman for the rest of the day. That's a win for the both of us. I establish that I expect to be treated in a certain way, and he gets a little boost, too.

Some girls are brought up to be Southern Belles, but that's not the only way to get there. I was certainly raised right by my mama, but I have refined the formula, and I keep working at it. Southern Belles never stop learning and improving; we are all masterpieces in progress. And I am convinced that every woman's life could be improved if she knew even a fraction of what I know. That's why I wrote *Secrets of the Southern Belle.* So let's imagine we're rocking on the porch, with a tall glass of sweet tea and a plate of ladyfingers and cucumber sandwiches. Listen up—I've got a thing or two to tell you.

Don't Let Geography Stand in Your Way

I don't want any of you nice people thinking that you have to live south of the Mason-Dixon Line in order to be a Southern Belle. Sure, it's easier—you'll have Belle role models all around you. But let me tell you, when a Belle swings into action outside of the South, she has incredible impact. I guess people just aren't used to our fun-loving package of looks, charm, and determination.

So go ahead and put my advice to work, wherever you live. I'm sure you'll enjoy the results. And if you can't get to the South, here are a few ways to bring the South to you.

∞ Have an indoor living-room "tailgate party" for your favorite Southeastern Conference (SEC) bowl game. Get pompoms and monogrammed beer-can cozies in school colors; serve sweet tea and pimiento cheese sandwiches.

∞ Wear pearls. Every day, if possible. Doesn't matter if they're real.

∞ Smile a lot and look everyone in the eye. I know some women in urban areas find this a challenge, so you might start with just an hour at a time.

∞ Use rubber gloves when you do the dishes. Belles always have pretty hands.

∞ Buy something pink, even if it's just a felt-tip pen.

∞ Surprise a gentleman of your acquaintance with an innocent but sincere compliment.

∞ Try a shoe with a higher heel.

∞ Decorate your home for the next holiday.

Be Nice

Everybody Knows . . .

It won't kill you to be nice.

° How to Be Nice °

I would like to believe that most people have good intentions, because, really, who actually wants the rest of the world to think they were raised by wolves? So I gladly give everyone credit for at least *trying* to behave well. However, the truth is, some people could use some extra help. If you ever have the pleasure of spending time in the South, you can readily note the fundamentally different way southerners interact with people. People who are not from the South are often confused or genuinely surprised when they experience true southern hospitality. Smiling, greeting strangers on the street, and opening doors are not common in all parts of the world. But it surely makes us happier people!

Our ability to be kind and generally respect others comes from most of us being raised under the biblical premise of "do unto others as you would have them do unto you." In the South, whether you live in downtown Atlanta or rural Alabama, there are no strangers. Most of us realize from early childhood that karma is real and the bridge you so easily burn might well be the bridge you have to cross to get home. In different parts of the world that move at a faster pace, being insensitive or considering most people as dispensable seems to be the norm. But in the South we treasure being respectable and respecting others. Unfortunately, as we see more migration from other parts of the world, we also see an increase of poor manners and rude behavior. But the Southern Belle prides herself on treating everyone like the next president, because potential is not always obvious; your parking valet today might be chairman of the city council tomorrow.

So we greet people. It's such a small thing, but I notice that in some cities, no one ever says hello, good morning, or have a nice day. They intentionally avoid making eye contact with any and all living things. (Apparently their shoes and belt buckles are quite the conversationalists!) I find it particularly odd in business, when the salespeople or tellers don't speak or thank you for your patronage. Don't they realize that without customers they would not have a job? I guess my mama's favorite adage, "Common sense isn't common," is definitely true in most cases. To intentionally ignore someone's presence is just simply rude; if someone pretends you don't exist for long enough, you might start believing them!

We say, "Hello, how are you doing today?" even if we have no interest in the answer. Everybody always says, "I'm fine, thanks for asking, and how are you?" We might mention the weather. When appropriate, a Belle will try to bring a compliment into the conversation. It's as simple as this: we treat the people we meet as human beings. We try to pay attention to them.

And I'd like to think we try to be considerate. We aren't in as much of a hurry, so we'll let somebody get in line in front of us if asked nicely. We are especially kind to the elderly and the infirm. We do favors for people. We are warm, but at the same time we are formal, which is why we are always well-groomed. Some of these habits, which some might consider old-fashioned—like writing notes and sending flowers—are very charming and endearing, as you will learn on your way to becoming a Southern Belle.

Everybody Knows . . .

You never show up anywhere empty-

handed, and you never leave a party

without thanking the host or hostess.

° What You Don't Know °

Here's something I've never quite understood about non-southerners. They're suspicious of basic southern warmth because they're worried it's insincere. But at the same time, they will tell you the most inappropriate things! They tell you stuff about their health that you don't want to know. They launch into these long crazy stories about their terrible childhoods and how misunderstood they are. They complain about what happened long ago, and they fret openly about the future. Then they tell you what they paid for things and you want to crawl under the table.

Frankly, that's not very attractive. In the South, we prefer to draw a veil over all that unpleasantness. And over a lot of other things as well. The Belle retains an aura of mystery to everyone but her very closest friends. She doesn't announce her projects before they are complete. She certainly doesn't share her family concerns with all and sundry. (My current pet peeve is money problems. I do *not* want to know how deep in debt and close to foreclosure you are, for heaven's sake!)

Don't Tell, Don't Ask

I am often astounded by the conversations I overhear outside of the South. Why does anyone discuss financial or digestive or sexual questions in detail in public? But there are people in this world who seem to feel that no inquiry is too intimate.

Honey, I am not one of them. And here's the remarkable thing that some folks don't understand: you do not have to answer the question you are asked! For instance:

Tactless Query	Belle's Answer
Have you gained weight?	Oh, honey, who weighs themselves? Got to leave something for the doctor to do.
Is your hair color natural?	That depends on what you mean by "natural"!
How old are you?	Old enough to vote. Unless you're the new administrator for Social Security checks.
Was that expensive?	My husband certainly thought so.
What do you think about [controversial subject]?	I'm sure there's a lot more to it than what we hear in the news.

The Belle glides through life with a smile and a cheerful greeting for everyone. She can chat with a dead man if she needs to. But her secret is that she's a great listener. She asks a lot more questions than she answers. So at the end of an evening with a Belle, you don't know a thing about her politics or her bank balance or who made her dress. The Southern Belle is a woman of mystery, and she likes it that way.

° *Speak Softly* °

One of the attractive features of the Southern Belle is the way she talks. I'm not necessarily referring to her accent, so you don't need to teach yourself to drawl. We do speak softly, though. Our mothers teach us from the start not to raise our voices. It's a much more effective way to communicate, because people have to get closer to you to hear what you have to say. The Southern Belle is always looking to establish a connection with people, and yelling is not helpful or attractive. You catch more flies with honey than with vinegar. That's the principle behind the way we talk down South.

∞ Be lavish with the compliments. I don't know why some people are so concerned with being sincere, when being nice is so much more effective.

∞ Never contradict anyone, even if you know they are wrong. Southern Belles shy away from needless confrontation. There's always a better way to reach your goal. So if someone tells you that your taxes are due on April 30 instead of April 15, you look puzzled and say, "Goodness, I had no idea. Did they change the date?"

∞ React! Watch a Southern woman listen and you'll know what I mean. She nods, she smiles, she says, "Really?" or "Mmm-hmmm" to encourage the speaker.

∞ Ask questions, of course. Don't worry if they're obvious, they put people at ease. Besides, there isn't a person alive who doesn't want to talk about himself or herself.

∞ Learn some new words. We use vivid language in the South; it's a culture of storytelling. Some of our expressions might be jarring in the North, but just the right word at the right time makes you worth listening to.

Compliments That Come in Handy

My, you look so refreshed, have you been away on vacation?

What an interesting way to think about it. (Good for a point on which you disagree with someone.)

Oh, this looks so delicious!

Your house looks beautiful, you must have been an interior designer in another life.

You really have a remarkable eye for color. Promise me you will let me borrow your eyes for my next project.

You thought of every little detail; I love a meticulous lady!

Wow! That is so original. I would have never put it together like that. (In the South this might mean, "I hate it," but in a polite way.)

That dress looks so pretty on you. If I didn't know any better I would have sworn the designer made it just for you.

That is so refreshing!

Everybody Knows . . .

Nobody really wants to hear

about your health, especially

female issues.

° *Talk the Talk* °

Of course you can tell when you're talking to a southern lady, but it's not just that many of us have an attractive regional accent. What we say is as important as how we say it. Sometimes northern women can sound awfully abrupt. It's just a habit they have, poor things.

For one thing, we naturally use terms of endearment. It's not unusual for me to address my friends as "honey." Sometimes to soften a blow I slip in something affectionate so that a very harsh reality doesn't come across as rude or abrupt. Like, "Darling, don't you know you're too smart and pretty to be the town drunk?"

We're very generous with compliments, too. Every time you see two southern women meet, they're going to spend a couple of minutes causing a commotion about each other's appearance. "Well, don't you look beautiful!" is just the start. If you can't find something nice to say about a friend's hair or clothes or shoes or manicure, you simply are not trying hard enough. You don't have to *mean* it, you know. In fact, if you can tell that someone has put a lot of effort into a particular aspect of her outfit, just draw attention to it. Sparkly stars-and-stripes high heels could be terribly tacky, but you bet they're supposed to be noticed, so go ahead and do it. "Those are certainly patriotic shoes!"

Every woman is gorgeous and every man is handsome, or dapper, or well dressed. The kind of man a Belle wants to be around makes an effort with his appearance and deserves to have that praised. I have noticed that some women are shy about paying obvious compliments to men. I say spread the love! If anyone needs the direct approach, it's a man. Men want their efforts noticed just as much as women.

Poor Thing

We understand that not everyone has the good fortune to be a Southern Belle. Some women haven't even been exposed to a Belle, so they aren't aware of all the advantages they're missing. This is why we look on them not with scorn but with pity. We try to be kind when we speak of them. You won't hear a Belle speak of a non-Belle or any woman as "that bitch," no, ma'am. Never. We don't use words like that. Instead, we'll say, "Poor thing." Or maybe, "Well, she tries." Or, "She doesn't know any better." About someone you can't stand, you might say, "We don't see eye to eye," or "She's just not my cup of tea." Then if you really want to emphasize your dislike, you might add, "Bless her heart."

Believe me, that will get your point across very clearly.

Take It from Me

Let's say I'm having a party and my neighbor Karen has a huge salad bowl I would like to borrow. First of all, she must be invited to the party. (Never, ever talk about a party you're giving to someone who isn't invited!) Then, a few days ahead of time, you call her up. The conversation might go like this:

Phaedra: "Good morning, Karen. How are you? Did I catch you at a good time?" (Of course I know that she prefers to make phone calls in the morning before her day gets busy.)

Karen: "Hi, Phaedra, of course it's a good time. How are you? How's the barbecue planning going? David and I are so looking forward to it. I hope you're making your potato salad! Are you going to let me bring something?"

Phaedra: "No, of course not, you just bring your sweet self and that handsome husband of yours."

Karen: "You sure? Anything I can do for you ahead of time? I'm running to the grocery store this afternoon, can I pick up some flowers for you?"

Phaedra: "Oh, you are too thoughtful! I'm all set on flowers. But there is one thing I am lacking—don't you have a nice big etched-crystal salad bowl? I thought I remembered seeing one last year at your party, am I remembering that right?"

Karen: "I sure do. You want me to drop it off right now? I'm about to leave the house."

Phaedra: "No, I wouldn't dare inconvenience you, I'm headed out myself. How about I pick it up on my way out or, if you like, you can leave it on your porch and I'll swing by and get it."

Karen: "No need to come all the way over here, I'll drop it on *your* porch."

Phaedra: "No, you most certainly won't, I'm walking out of the house right now to get it. I need the exercise more than you!"

After this polite little fuss about who has the pleasure of picking up or delivering the bowl, you make a decision and everyone is happy. (And by the way, if I ever borrow a bowl or a dish, I return it spotlessly clean with something in it, like a dozen clementines or a batch of cookies.) Yes, this conversation could take half as much time if all we cared about was efficiency. But that's not who we are down South.

We also assume that everyone's time is extremely valuable. If you call anyone other than a very good friend on the phone, you say, "Did I reach you at a good time? I know how busy you are." And the Southern Belle way to end a call is to say, "This has been so helpful/interesting/entertaining, but I'll let you get back to your busy schedule." "Thanks, I appreciate you taking the time to speak with me" is a phrase I end up using a lot.

Here's another southern difference: we try not to make direct requests. It just sounds so forward and frankly unpleasant if someone comes right out and says what they want from you.

Everybody Knows . . .
A polite email is not the
same as a thank-you note
on pretty stationery.

° *Translation, Please* °

I am always amazed at how blunt some people are. It seems like they'll say anything that pops into their heads. We handle things a little differently down South, though. We manage to communicate how we feel about people without being obviously catty. For instance, if I tell someone "Goodness, you must have spent all day on your hair. I am so impressed!" it really means I hate it. If I see someone walking past me looking disheveled, I just say, "Bless her heart." That basically means, "She is so pitiful, honey." Or I might say, "God bless her." Basically that means that it would take divine intervention or a magician to make that woman into a Southern Belle.

And when you're discussing a homely girl, you generally say, "She's so smart!" The general thought is you can't be both ugly and dumb. God wouldn't be that cruel.

Belle-Speak	_Unvarnished Truth_
She's such a free spirit.	She's a tramp.
She's quite the charmer.	She's a sneaky liar.
Eccentric.	A total weirdo.
Very particular, persnickety.	A pain in the butt.
He's finding himself.	He's unemployed.
That's a healthy girl.	She's obese.
Isn't she busy!	She's a busybody.
She's never at a loss for words.	She talks way too much.
You are casket-ready.	You are dressed impeccably today.
I hope the baby looks like his dad.	Paternity is questionable.
She brought the party with her.	She's a drunk hot mess.
I hope she's smart.	She's very unattractive.
Thank God she's pretty.	She's as dumb as a doorknob.
He's light in the loafers.	He's gay.
She models shoes.	She's a stripper.
She's a lady of leisure.	She doesn't have a job.
She's an ambitious girl.	She's a gold digger.
She's a nurse-in-training.	She dates only old men.
She's a professional dater.	She's an escort/prostitute.
She's a butter face.	Everything looks good but her face.
Hope he's got money.	He's unattractive and pays for affection.
He needs to eat a pizza.	He is extremely skinny.

° *Irresistible Conversation Starters* °

A Southern Belle never meets a stranger. In other words, we become easily acquainted with everyone we meet. Even the most bashful woman in the South can get a conversation started and keep it going. However, I understand that what comes so naturally to us may not be obvious to everyone, so here are some suggestions.

The best icebreaker is a smile. Don't wait to be introduced; if you just walk up to someone with your hand extended and say, "I'm Phaedra, it is so nice to meet you," well, good things will happen!

Sometimes you greet someone cheerfully and they don't know what to say next. This is not a problem. *You* continue the conversation with another statement or open-ended question. Easy ones: "How was your ride over here?" "The weather looks good, but I think I heard a storm is coming. Have you heard or seen the news?" Everybody's a little nervous when meeting strangers, so don't throw them complicated or controversial subjects like politics, animal rights, or local zoning. You're not even trying to be interesting: just calm them down. The next question should be a follow-up on something your new acquaintance just said. You're trying to *find common ground*: Do you have friends who know each other? Have you ever lived in the same town? Visited the same city?

Take It from Me

Sometimes it's disarming to make light of the anxiety in the situation. I might say I was worried that I would be the only person wearing a certain look or that I don't usually go to this kind of party. You're creating a rapport, and it eventually loosens people up. I just keep on talking until they pick up the conversation, and they always do sooner or later. I met one of my best friends this way, in my bar review class. She looked fun, and on the first day I asked her if she'd brought lunch. She just said no. Every question I asked got a monosyllabic answer. Well, I just kept asking questions and wouldn't let her eat lunch alone and we laugh about it to this day. I later found out that Katrina, like me, was from a small town, the only difference being was she was raised in the Midwest (Finley, Ohio) and I was reared in the South. She said I reminded her of a Scarlett O'Hara dipped in chocolate. After we became close friends, she confided in me that she had never met anyone so nice and insistent on being her friend. And now, we have been cozier than socks in January for almost fifteen years, so it works.

Still not getting anywhere? Okay, this person is seriously shy. You're going to need to do some of the talking just to get them warmed up. Don't worry about sounding interesting. "Interesting" is an overrated notion. Just fill the empty air. Comment on your host and hostess, how nice they are, how attractive the house is. *Keep it all positive*. Negative remarks are intimidating.

I'm not a comparison shopper when it comes to party conversation. You know those people who are always glancing over your shoulder to see who else they should be talking to? No, ma'am, I don't believe in that. I would rather *focus 100 percent* on one person at a time, even if I don't know who that person is. You never know who is going to turn out to have a fascinating story.

After you have made your mark, keep it moving, and *make new acquaintances*. Simply say: "I have so enjoyed getting to know you. I hope we speak again, but I need to have a word with our hostess/my husband. It was definitely a pleasure meeting you tonight, stay in touch." And you're off to the next adventure. I am sure you can sound like you mean it, right?

Everybody Knows . . .

A lady doesn't raise her voice

or point her finger.

° *Never Say No* °

One difference between northern and southern manners is that we take a little more time getting where we're going. This applies to our conversations, too. For instance, you will rarely hear a southern woman say an outright no. Even if you ask a simple question like, "Do you happen to know what time it is?" she'll say something such as, "I'm so sorry, I didn't wear a watch today."

I'm sure they mean well, but some women I've met north of the Mason-Dixon Line can be blunt to the point of being abrupt! I'm sure if they could hear themselves they'd want to get in the habit of using phrases like these:

Q: Would you like another cup of coffee?
A: I would drink the whole pot, but in the interest of all I will limit myself.

Q: Have you seen the latest Sandra Bullock movie?
A: Not yet, but I'm sure it's Oscar worthy. Have you?

Q: Do you want to meet for a lunch tomorrow?

A: I would love to, but unfortunately I am in meetings all day.

Q: Do you like grilled octopus?

A: I love it, but lately it hasn't liked me or my stomach.

Q: Would you like to live in Boston?

A: Boston is a wonderful city with a lot of history, but my heart belongs to Atlanta.

Everybody Knows . . .

You spoon soup away

from you.

° Table Manners °

There are a lot of strange ideas out there about good manners. Some people seem to think that etiquette is all about one person acting superior and making everyone else feel ignorant, but it's exactly the opposite. Good manners are supposed to make the people around you feel comfortable. However, table manners can present a challenge, especially if you've had the pleasure of attempting to teach a young child how to use a knife and fork. If you can survive this battle, you realize table manners don't come naturally.

But good table manners aren't all about being finicky and fussy and sticking your little finger up in the air when you drink a cup of tea. They're really about getting food neatly into your mouth while also helping to keep a pleasant conversation going. Meals are an important time for socializing as well as for fueling up. So the Southern Belle isn't trying to attract attention with her flashy knife skills. At mealtime, she wants to enjoy the cuisine; eat discreetly, so she doesn't distract anyone; and promote lively chat. In the end, it's the personal connections that are going to be memorable, much more than whether she knew how to use a finger bowl. (She does, of course. See "Advanced Table Manners" on page 35.)

∞ Put away the phone, and turn off the TV. I hate sitting down at a table with people who put their BlackBerries next to their plates (I have on occasion been guilty of this myself, but I try to avoid it at all costs). The people in front of you are what's important, unless you're expecting to be called in to perform an urgent organ transplant.

∞ Sit back in your chair, and put your napkin in your lap. Don't lean forward and put an arm around your plate as if you expect someone to snatch it away from you. It's all yours, darling, and you can consume it at your leisure. I haven't heard of any cases of plate-napping in many moons; I think most thieves prefer to pilfer the silverware.

∞ Chew with your mouth closed, and don't talk until you've swallowed. We all tend to think that what we have to say is fascinating, but most of the time it can actually wait a few seconds. My mama used to tell us we were like cows chomping on their cud if we made smacking noises while eating (this is also true for gum chewers).

∞ There are all kinds of ways to talk about how you should hold your knife and fork, but the basic point is that you don't grab them in your closed fists. They're tools, like a pencil, not weapons.

∞ Don't reach. If the bread basket is across the table, ask someone to pass it to you ("Please pass the corn-bread."). Make sure you wait until there's a break in the conversation. Being a Southern Belle is all about self-control.

∞ Don't make a fuss, unless you're complimenting the cook. "Oh, my goodness, after eating your red vel-vet cake I'm ready to die and go to heaven" is the right kind of fuss. And if it is the best you have ever had you should say, "Girl, you put your foot in this," which means she gave it everything she had and then some more. "Is there meat in here? I'm a vegetarian" is the wrong kind of fuss. If you don't have a medical condition, you should just eat around anything you can't identify or don't like.

∞ Don't ask for something that nobody has offered you unless you're at a restaurant. If the hostess says, "light or dark meat?" that's your choice, and don't go looking for some third option like rib eye.

∞ Always wait for your host or hostess to start eating. This is a good idea if you aren't exactly sure how to handle certain foods or utensils. Notice how the hostess handles it, and copy her. You will never go wrong this way. You'll also never be embarrassed by looking up from your plate to realize that only half the table has been served and you're almost done with your soup.

∞ Remember that napkin you put in your lap when you sat down? Use it often but discreetly. Don't swipe it across your face like a towel at the gym.

∞ There are subjects we don't discuss at the dinner table. This Southern Belle doesn't want to mention them in print, but you can probably figure out what they are. Rule of thumb: if you wouldn't discuss it in the presence of your parents with your pastor at the table, then save that topic for a more appropriate time and place.

∞ Mealtimes are social, so we may linger for a while when we've finished eating. Let someone else be the first to make a move away from the table. It is never cute to eat and run.

∞ Unless there's professional staff around, help the hostess clear the table. Offer to help in the kitchen between courses, and if you see anything that obviously needs to be taken care of, just do it without any fuss. When the meal is finished, offer again to assist in cleanup. No cook wants to wake up to a dirty kitchen.

∞   Always compliment the cook!

Everybody Knows . . .

Plates are always taken

away from the right:

"Leave left, remove right."

° Advanced Table Manners °

In the last section I covered some rules for basic table manners, but I know many Southern Belles are ready for the advanced course. Many peculiar foods have to be eaten in unusual ways (artichokes and oysters, to name just two). There are also elaborate ways to set a table and they could be intimidating if you have never encountered them before. Most of the time, though, the following simple rules will keep you straight.

If all else fails, remember the secret weapon of the Southern Belle is delicate helplessness. Confused by the table setting in front of you? Turn to

Pearl of Wisdom

Here's a little trick to help you when you set a table. Make an "okay" sign with your left hand; your fingers make a lowercase "b," which indicates the side for the bread plate. Now make an "okay" sign with your right hand; your fingers make a lowercase "d," which indicates the side for the drink.

the gentleman at your side and just ask him discreetly for his advice. Even if he doesn't know anything more than you do, at least the two of you will be wrong together.

∞ Work from the outside in. If you sit down at a table and each place setting seems to have ten pieces of cutlery, relax. Watch your hostess to see what she does, but the basic rule is that you pick up the implement farthest from your plate first. So that big spoon is for soup, that little fork for salad, the big fork and knife for the main course. Some fine restaurants make a point of having all kinds of funny-shaped special forks or knives for specific dishes, such as fish forks or risotto spoons. Servers will bring these once you've ordered. Just follow the pattern: outside in.

∞ Spoon your soup toward the center of the table, away from you. Actually this is practical, too—you won't spill soup in your lap. And *never* slurp!

∞ When you're finished, put your fork and knife side by side on your plate, with the blade of the knife facing the fork. If you think about clearing the plate, that's easier to remember: the blade can't cut the waiter. It's the same reason why we leave spoons on the saucer of a bowl or cup. There's less danger that whoever clears the table might spill all over the guests.

∞ Don't worry about the glasses. Sometimes at a banquet or a formal wedding each place is set with as many as four glasses. But you know what? It's not your job to fill them! All you have to do is drink out of the one you want. Normally the wines at a fine meal will progress from white to red, maybe extending to champagne with dessert, but you can drink whatever you want whenever you want—as long as you don't overdo it.

∞ Try to talk to the people on both sides of you. (See page 22 for irresistible conversation starters.) If you've started a conversation with one neighbor, but the other one seems to be at loose ends, try to include both of them. Introduce them to each other and explain your subject: "Jason, Roger and I were just talking about his collection of antique cars. He has one of those cars James Bond used to drive." If you're lucky they'll talk to each other and you can concentrate on your meal.

∞ If you encounter a finger bowl, you've gotten into pretty elevated company—or high cotton as we say in the South. I think finger bowls are pretentiously perfect! But since few people are very familiar with them, they can be very intimidating. Sometimes they do appear at the end of a meal, just before dessert.

Of course you'll be on the safe side if you just watch your hostess. Don't drink the water in the bowl! Just dabble your fingers in it, wipe them on your napkin, and lift the bowl and doily beneath it (if there is one) off your plate. Put them on the table in front of you. The waiter will remove them.

∞ Don't lose track of what you're drinking. Sometimes you'll be in a setting where your glass keeps getting refilled. If you don't want more wine, it's fine to shake your head or cover your glass. You can even have the waiter take it away. The Belle doesn't ever want to get inebriated in public.

° *Just a Note* °

If there's any characteristic that defines a Southern Belle, it's her habit of firing off little notes on any occasion. We don't just have a box of note cards in our desks: we have an entire wardrobe of stationery for various occasions, along with all kinds of cute stamps and specialty pens. Southern Belles practically keep the US Postal Service in business.

The primary unit of Southern Belle correspondence is the thank-you note. We learn about this early. As soon as a child can write, she's expected to cheerfully sit down with her personalized stationery and write out her thanks for any gifts and or niceties she receives. Really strict mothers usually will not let a present be worn or played with until that note is in the mail.

When you're an adult, you absolutely must thank your hostess in writing every time you are entertained. Not if you're just sitting in the kitchen with a glass of tea—we are polite but not neurotic! But for any event that required planning and effort, you have to get out your pen and paper. In the era of email and texts some people think that electronic communication is adequate, but that opinion definitely does not wash with a true Southern Belle. It is fine to dash off an email when you get home just because we're all so used to instant communication. But you wouldn't want your hostess to think for a moment that her efforts weren't appreciated. The email is just a warm-up: the paper note must always follow. And follow *fast*. While it would be great to complete your thank-you note the moment you arrive home, everybody knows the modern day Southern Belle is inundated with so many tasks that once she gets home there is another pressing task awaiting her. However, a thank-you note should arrive in a prompt fashion in most cases. I have heard of women who write notes in advance so they're ready, stamped, and addressed to go in the mail the next day. But you don't want to be like the woman I've heard of who sent a thank-you note for a holiday dinner that accidentally got mailed with a pile of Christmas cards. The hostess received it the morning *before* her party. That could only happen to an overzealous Southern Belle.

Now, some thank-you notes are better than others. Beginning your note with, "Thank you for . . ." is amateurish. A personal statement sounds so much better. Try something like, "We had such a wonderful time at your dinner last night," or "You're so kind to remember my birthday." Always mention something specific about the event or gift. Comment on the food ("I have never had such tasty okra") or the guests ("You were so sweet to seat me next to your grandfather") or the entertainment ("I've always been curious about professional yodeling"). Obviously it's perfectly all right to exaggerate. Then you can end with the thank-you.

The other kind of letter every Southern Belle writes a lot is the condolence note. It doesn't have to be complicated. All you're aiming to do is let the bereaved person know that you're thinking about him or her. You can start by saying, "I was so sorry to hear about your loss" or "your stepsister's passing" or whatever fits the purpose. The middle section is the challenge. If you have personal memories of the deceased, share them. "Your mother was always so elegant," or "I loved your friend Joe's Texas tall tales"—that kind of thing. If you didn't know the deceased, a statement such as "hopefully the fond times you shared with your father will bring you peace." In closing it's always appropriate to offer prayers and comfort. Most people just want you to acknowledge the loss of their loved one.

Sometimes if I'm not sure exactly what I want to say, I'll write out a quick first draft. I don't want to get a note partly written on my pretty stationery and realize that I can't figure out how to end a particular sentence. And these notes should look lovely: best handwriting, correctly spaced on the page, no crossing out, and no misspelled words or correction fluid.

One lesson my mama taught me is to make a habit of letting people know how important they are to you. So I often end up writing a little note to a friend just to say that I'm thinking about her. It doesn't take much longer than texting, if you have a box of nice notes in your desk. One sentence will do. Just wait till you get a note like that in the mail—it's a full-strength dose of southern charm in an envelope.

Pen and Paper

Every Southern Belle has her stash of writing paper, with different papers for different occasions. You can't write a condolence note on a fluorescent starburst card. That would give the wrong impression. But you also don't want to send a get-well card on your most formal stationery or your friend will think she's headed to the grave.

What you write *with* matters, too. Never, ever write a letter in pencil. You might as well not bother at all. Ink is essential. I'm partial to different-colored fine-point felt-tip markers that can complement or contrast with the color of my paper. Blue or black are perfectly acceptable, even if they do lack panache. Blots and smearing are terrible, though. You just can't send something that isn't pretty and polished.

∞   Note cards: I always stop in museum gift shops to pick up a box of cards. These are perfect for a thank-you after a luncheon, or a little "how are you, I miss you" note. Sometimes you can get small museum cards that also work as enclosures for gifts. They're hard to find, so stock up!

∞ Personalized paper: Every Southern Belle has her own stationery, either monogrammed or embossed with her name. I have both and some more options, too. Folding cards are perfect for thank-you notes because there isn't a whole lot of writing space. The embossing goes on the front. You might have sheets, too, maybe with your first name and last name, for more businesslike correspondence such as your volunteer work. Some of my note cards have my name and my husband's so I can write notes for both of us. (Men tend not to see the need for a thank-you note.) I love pink paper, so I have a lot of it, but you do always need a box of gray or white paper so you can write a sober condolence letter.

∞ Holiday cards: Oh, darling! Holiday cards are huge in the South! I know people who get and send several hundred every year. Sometimes it seems like everyone they ever met is on their card list. This can turn into a really big production. First you need the right card, which typically is a professionally taken photograph or a collage of pictures of your lovely family, including the dog. I know some families that schedule an annual photo shoot every summer. They get everyone into some color- and style-coordinated outfit and pose on the beach, in front of the mantel, porch of their house, or in their yard amid magnolia trees and lush flowers. Then once the pictures are chosen and the card designed and printed, the Belle sits down at her dining room table to sign, address, and send them all out. Please use holiday stamps— and I often receive cards that require extra postage, so that's an extra step right there: ordering the special stamps from the post office weeks in advance.

I'm not crazy about the long letters some people include with their holiday cards. For one thing, a printed document folded up and tucked into a pretty card distracts from the beauty of the card itself, and for another thing, people do get carried away with their family news—I love to see updated photos of everyone, but I don't need to know every soccer game that was won and how many times the school called you about Parker's ability to see through walls. If everyone was really as successful, gifted, and happy as those letters say, churches and psychiatrists' offices would be empty.

° Giving and Getting °

You want to know one of the nicest things about being a Southern Belle? We get lots of gifts. Now I wouldn't want you to think this is a one-way arrangement; we love to give gifts, too. It's the same thing with all the little notes we send around, or dropping in to visit with a friend. These are all ways we stay connected in the South.

I know I'm not the only woman who stocks up on cute items so I always have just the right gift on hand. You just never know when someone's going to go out of their way for you—and you want them to know it's appreciated. Of course I keep track of the birthdays and anniversaries of friends, colleagues, and my whole family, as well as Hanukkah and Christmas—well, Christmas is a huge deal. I shop for Christmas all year long.

Choosing the right gift is sharing a little bit of yourself, so the gifts you give should reflect your individual character. I like to give thoughtful, personalized items, but I know women who are great at crafts and sewing who make wonderful gifts as well. I'd like to be the kind of friend who could knit a little hat and booties for a new baby, but since I was never still enough as a youngster, my aunt was unable to pass down the craft.

A gift should also be appropriate to the occasion. What works for a preschool teacher at the end of the year isn't the same as what works for a girlfriend's fortieth birthday. And as for giving gifts across the gender divide: well, good luck. Sometimes it's nice to give something to a male business associate, but you'd want to keep it pretty impersonal. Tickets to a game or concert, or maybe a beautiful crystal mug.

Presentation is very important. If I were giving a man a pair of tickets to an Atlanta Falcons game, I wouldn't just stick them in an envelope. I might find a jersey or a cap with the Falcons logo and tuck the tickets inside as a nice surprise. I stock up on wrapping paper and ribbons and gift cards so I can always dress up a gift for any occasion. Even if the present itself is modest, glamorous paper and a decadent bow give it standout curb appeal.

Have I ever received a gift I didn't much like? No, because I'm always touched by the effort. Everybody knows it is the thought that counts. There may have been some items of clothing that weren't quite the right size or the right color (usually purchased by well-meaning but misguided gentlemen). You do what you can to make them wearable and make sure you're seen at least once in whatever it was. From time to time something leaves my house to find a new home in an undisclosed location, but only if the person who gave it will never find out. I hear that there are places where "regifting parties" are all the rage, but no Southern Belle would be interested in that kind of social event.

And I'm sure I don't need to point this out, but every gift deserves a written thank-you note.

° *Always the Bridesmaid* °

Who complains about being selected as a bridesmaid? Not the Southern Belle, I assure you. This is one of the greatest compliments anyone can pay you, and if you don't like being singled out as one of the dearest friends of the bride, I can't imagine what *would* make you happy.

Anyway, the duties of the bridesmaid fall right into the Southern Belle's area of expertise: looking elegant, behaving like a lady, and making sure everyone else has a good time. Here are some do's and don'ts especially for this occasion.

o   *Do* be enthusiastic. Sometimes bridesmaids get invited to a plethora of parties for the bride. There's often a bachelorette weekend, showers, brunches, teas, and a rehearsal dinner. Yes, we all have jobs, and yes, the groomsmen may be lame or just silly dorks. A great bridesmaid goes to every event with a smile on her face and a gift in her hand. She talks to the groom's grandmother and dances with the nephew from out of town.

- *Don't* complain. About the dress, about your bouquet, about the bar prices, about the early call for hair and makeup. Act as if everything is just exactly the way you would choose it to be. If you are not happy, simply pretend to be.

- *Do* be helpful. Drive to the airport to pick up guests? Hold the mirror? Address envelopes? Make sure the bride gets to every single one of those Zumba classes? Yes, ma'am, certainly, I'd love to.

- *Don't* get drunk. Ladies, what we see on movie screens doesn't represent reality. You know that, don't you? And even if it did, would you want to be the bridesmaid who decided to remove her strapless bra on the dance floor? The Southern Belle has nothing against a festive occasion, but she can have fun without getting sloppy, and she definitely never embarrasses herself or her friends.

- *Do* wear waterproof mascara. Test it in the shower.

- *Do* break in your shoes ahead of time.

- *Do* write thank-you notes to the hostess of every party and the manager/owner of the venue.

- *Do* your very best to make sure the bride has a wonderful time. A wedding is a momentous occasion and bridesmaids aren't there just to make a pretty background for the girl in the white dress. You're her emotional support. Do your job!

° *First Things First* °

Visitors to the South always notice how well behaved our children are. Of course there are plenty of little monsters south of the Mason-Dixon Line, but a little Southern Belle or Southern Gentleman is raised up right by her or his Southern Belle mother. I won't deceive you, this is a lot of work. There are no shortcuts to good habits! But these habits are the building blocks of good manners. They're nonnegotiable.

∞ Yes, *who*? Southerners say "yes, ma'am; no, ma'am; yes, sir; no, sir." These are short words, one syllable, and there is no reason in the world your precious little toddlers can't say them if you keep after them. Actually once they say it you'll see there's nothing cuter in the whole world. You'll want to make sure they make it a habit.

∞ Please and thank you. Same deal; if a child can talk, she can say "please" and "thank you." Just keep after them.

∞ We sit down at meals. I have heard—though I find it hard to believe—that in some families the little ones are free to eat wherever they want, whenever they want. No, ma'am, that is *not* happening in a good ole southern household. This seems pretty elementary, but maybe I need to spell it out: we all sit down at once, around a table, which has been set with plates and cutlery and glasses and napkins. (They don't have to be fine porcelain and linen, by the way; Belles love to set a pretty table but let's be realistic about what's possible in family life!) We say grace, and we enjoy our meal together with the television and hopefully all phones turned off. My goodness, we even talk to one another! The little ones ask to be excused, and their little bottoms need to stay in their chairs until Mama says they may get down from the table. If they start to fidget, it could take longer.

∞ Basic table manners are essential. Of course it's easier to just let the little ones grab the food with their fingers and chew with their mouths open, but their adult social lives are going to be pretty limited if they can't acquire better habits. Napkins go in their laps. They chew and swallow before speaking. They don't reach for food but ask for it: "May I have more soufflé, please?"

∞ Children eat what they are given. The southern mama doesn't like to see her labor go to waste, and she's not a short-order cook. Your toddler doesn't like greens? Better luck tomorrow.

∞ Actually, grown-ups are more important than children. That's why we get to sit in the comfortable chairs, choose the TV channel, and have conversations that don't get interrupted. Unless someone is bleeding or having a fit. Even so, a child breaking into an adult conversation won't be heard unless she says, "Excuse me, please."

∞ Children shake hands with adults and call them "mister" or "miss." That may seem awfully formal,

Straying from the Fold

Believe it or not, sometimes Southern Belles choose to forget their heritage and all of the good habits they learned growing up. They start saying to themselves, "Oh, that's just a southern thing," and they stop cleaning behind the refrigerator or curling their hair and wearing mascara. You might even hear them swearing in public, and they definitely neglect their wardrobes.

But the door is always open for these women to return; we're good people and we accept everyone. Especially if there are no trashy tattoos involved.

but at least it's clear. Even when an adult says, "Please use my first name," she should be addressed as "Ms. Phaedra."

∞ When you're a guest, you're on your best behavior. We understand that good manners take time to learn, and there's going to be some give and take as the little ones get the hang of the rules. But when a child goes to someone else's house, there's no slack at all.

° *The Little Guest* °

We're always in and out of each other's houses in the South, but that doesn't mean we aren't constantly aware of being guests and hosts. The thing to remember about us is that while we're warm, we are formal. We expect the niceties to be observed, even among our closest friends. And those expectations apply to children, too.

Things have changed since I grew up. When I was a youngster and my parents had guests over, we were expected to be seen and not heard. We couldn't even stay in the living room and listen quietly to the adults. Nowadays parents make more provisions for children, planning social events so that everyone has fun. But when a child crosses your threshold in the South, she's expected to abide by these rules.

∞ Address your host or hostess politely. If you're introduced to someone new, shake hands and look them in the eye.

∞ Don't go wandering around the house without permission. If you need the restroom, ask politely: "May I go wash my hands, Mrs. Parks?"

∞ Don't touch anything without being invited to. Not the dog, not the vase of flowers, not the pretty brocade chair.

∞ It's all right to ask for a glass of water but nothing else.

∞ You can accept what the hostess offers, but you can't ask for any substitutions, whether it's a drink or an activity.

∞ No southern child would ever consider saying she didn't like something. That's just plain rude.

∞ When you leave, thank your hostess and tell her what a nice time you had.

A child who follows these rules will grow into an adult who everyone's happy to see at the front door.

° Southern Belle No-No's °

There are certain things that a Southern Belle would never do, under any circumstances. They might seem strange to a northerner, but we have our reasons!

∞ Don't cross your legs at the knees—it promotes varicose veins. Cross them at the ankles instead.

∞ Don't ask anybody's age if they're obviously over eighteen. You can't do it legally in the job market, and you can't do it politely in a social setting. You can speculate about it, of course, as long as you're out of earshot. Anyway, the Southern Belle is ageless, unless you went to high school with her. Then you're in on the same secret.

∞ Don't arrive at a party without an RSVP. If you have ever *given* a party you should know to reply to the invitation even if you are not attending, so the hostess can be sure she has enough food and drink. That is just basic manners.

∞ Don't discuss the cost of anything. Any discussion of cost is just in poor taste. These days, if you aren't the Rockefellers you could be in the poorhouse at any second and the repo man will come for all your fancy toys.

∞ Don't discuss hair color. Men always pretend they don't dye their hair, so you just have to go with it. For women, it's a little bit more complicated because you have the question of whether the drapes match the carpet, so to speak. And I do know some who dye the carpet to match—that was the big thing in high school. Now with all this weird waxing, you don't have to do as much dyeing, but that's another thing you don't talk about either!

∞ Don't fix your makeup or adjust your wardrobe in public. I have actually seen women peel off their false eyelashes at the table. My eyes just about popped out of my head, and nobody ate another bite after that. And fishing in private places for straps to hoist our bodies back into place isn't appealing either. That's what the ladies' room is for.

And then there are the truly shocking breaches of good manners that you sometimes hear about. I think of these as the "She did *what*?" mistakes.

1. Changing the place cards at a seated dinner.

2. Wearing white to another woman's wedding.

3. Bringing a guest to an event, unless you were asked to.

4. Showing up to an event uninvited and complaining.

5. Asking a woman if she is pregnant. What if the answer is no?

6. Drinking beer from a bottle.

Work Hard

Everybody Knows . . .

It's not what you say but

how you say it.

° *How to Work Hard* °

Okay, since you've stuck with me this long, I'm going to let you in on a secret. I love to say that everything the Southern Belle does is seamless: you never see her sweat. But you and I know that actually nothing gets accomplished without exertion, right? The truth is that the Belle works all the time, even when she's having fun. She's just so used to it, she doesn't notice.

When I say "work," I mean "make an effort." Belles are not workaholics. We can leave the office behind. But you cannot be a Southern Belle if you are lazy. There's just too much that needs to get done during the day. And it has to get executed to a high standard. Anybody can get dressed for the office so she won't scare the folks in the neighboring cubicles, but if you've held down a job, you know that looking wonderful at 8:30 a.m. five days a week is a feat.

Consistency is part of the package. Who is always sitting in the same pew at church by the time the preacher enters, with her hair done and her children immaculately dressed and even better behaved? Who always delivers a presentation on time, with the printed materials perfectly written and proofread? Whose Christmas cards arrive the day after Thanksgiving, year after year? You know it, that's got to be a Southern Belle.

And she's as identifiable for what she doesn't do as for what she does. The Belle may like a glass of wine from time to time, but there won't ever be photos of her dancing on a tabletop. She may have a sense of humor that leans toward the risqué and a similar vocabulary, but she keeps them under wraps most of the time. (We cut loose now and then—as long as it's not documentable.) She makes the choice that works for the long term.

It does take a lot of discipline, but I am here to tell you discipline can be learned, one decision at a time. All day long we make choices, right? The Belle tries to make hers constructive. Just about the worst thing your mother can call you is lazy, so you might hear her voice in your head when you decide you can get away with not ironing your skirt, or not taking your makeup off and moisturizing before bed. (Belles usually avoid the "get away with" option.) We don't think of ourselves as driven, because that sounds so neurotic and unpleasant. But there is definitely an ideal of behavior we aspire to.

Take It from Me

No one is perfect, not even the Southern Belle. Lord, I can't even begin to tell you the mistakes I have made. For instance, I have a pretty hot temper and it's taken me a long time to get it under control. I do sometimes take my child to Chick-fil-A instead of cooking him dinner. And I have actually, believe it or not, driven to the nail salon without putting on my mascara first. A few times I have used some choice words that aren't in the Bible. The point is, we keep trying, every day, to live up to the Southern Belle ideal.

° The Lady °

Who wouldn't want to be a lady in this day and age? Don't we all want to be rare and unusual and cherished? Don't we want to appeal to men and women, and look forward to becoming a grande dame (see page 235)?

Well, you only have to turn on a TV set to know that lots of women make a different choice. But I think their lives would be better if they were Southern Belles, and you cannot be a Southern Belle unless you understand what it is to be ladylike.

I know the concept is old-fashioned. A lot of women today enjoy being the feisty, brassy, foul-mouthed kind of gal who drinks with the men and shows a lot of flesh. They think it's cool. And some women are almost afraid of being more feminine because they think they won't be taken seriously. Aggression replaces self-control.

That is certainly one model of womanhood. I've heard the argument that this is progress, from the feminist point of view, but I don't necessarily agree. Women do have more opportunities than they used to, but look at the reality: we're working harder than the men for less pay and less appreciation. Women have the jobs *and* they cook and clean, and who did that help? We made ourselves superwomen for no apparent reason. Being a Southern Belle corrects the balance, by restoring some of the appreciation. And some of the mystery.

Mind you, being a Belle isn't an act. It's true that there's an element of performance in everyday life, but the Belle's habits and ladylike behavior come naturally to her. They're all about self-respect. She owes it to herself to be nice and look pretty and think a step or two ahead of the situation where she finds herself.

So what exactly is a lady? How do you know one when you meet her?

She is always pleasant. She might loathe you, but you'll never know it. Well, another southern girl might understand that her elaborate politeness is the opposite of friendliness, but there will never be anything overt to object to.

She never loses her temper. I suppose a lady might raise her voice if she were in danger of being attacked, but the ability to remain composed is essential. If you feel like you're losing your cool, you remove yourself from a situation, like a toddler taking a time-out. You can always say, in a civil tone, "I need to end this conversation right now" and leave. You can take up where you left off later, after apologizing. If you lose control, you put yourself at a disadvantage. No one ever sees a lady sweat.

She looks as if she's heard of sex, probably has had sex, but has no plans to have sex with anybody in the immediate surroundings. I see women all over the place who look like they're just up for grabs. A lady never puts in the shop window what isn't for sale.

She doesn't cuss and doesn't talk dirty. Among her very closest friends, a lady may share secrets, but they won't get around. On the other hand, if somebody tells a good dirty joke in her vicinity, she'll laugh. A lady doesn't have to be prissy. She knows the vocabulary of a seasoned sailor, but she prides herself in being a wordsmith.

She keeps drinking to a minimum. I realize I'm a little bit strict about this. Coming from a Pentecostal family, I hate to see a woman down more than two drinks. I don't ever go to the bar at a party; I think that just looks terrible. If I must have a glass of wine or crave a fruity adult libation, I'll ask a nearby man to procure it for me. And much as I love a margarita, I don't have them often. When a Southern Belle cuts loose, even that happens in moderation. She's always thinking about the next day.

She's happy to ask for help. Asking for assistance doesn't mean you're helpless; it means that you hold the rest of the world to a high standard. You expect to be respected and treated properly. I have friends who have never in their lives pumped gas for their cars. They will ask a complete stranger to do it for them. One of my besties from New Orleans will flag down a man, give him her credit card, and have him pump and pay for her gas. Being a lawyer, I'm way too suspicious to give a stranger my credit card, so I have to ask my husband or some other gentlemen I know to pump my gas. I never carry my own suitcase, even in New York. Sometimes when I'm at a grocery store the fellow bagging the groceries will ask if he can take them out to my car. *Why would you say no to this?* But sometimes women do. And I look at them and sigh and think, "Poor thing. She has a lot to learn." (See "A Crash Course in Being [Selectively] Helpless" on page 70.)

° *The Power of Persuasion* °

One of the Belle's greatest assets in the workplace and else-where is her ability to get her way without getting in anyone's way. I've seen plenty of women try to bulldoze through a situation by shouting or pouting, but those tactics use up a lot of goodwill. I've learned a lot from some of the crafty Belles in my life who manage to be convincing without ever raising their voices. They:

∞ listen more than they talk.

∞ ask questions until they understand everybody's motivation.

∞ pay attention to body language and tone of voice.

∞ prefer a suggestion to a command.

∞ never give up (they just find another angle).

Take It from Me

For instance, my dear husband, Apollo, was not at all convinced that I should train as a funeral director. I see this as a way to establish a wonderful family business, but Apollo was dragging his feet. I didn't try to change his mind: I just signed up for full-time mortuary science school. Bit by bit, he got used to seeing my textbooks around our house and listening to my lectures. Of course, if this is going to be a family concern, he's going to need a significant role in it. I thought he might be interested in the embalming process, but let me tell you, when I took him to the funeral home I could barely get him through the door. That was obviously not a good fit! It turned out that what he really enjoyed was the fleet of vehicles for the funeral procession. Does he think the whole thing was his idea? Yes. Do I just smile and agree? Yes, indeed. And this way we're both happy. I can do all the things he considers "dirty work" and he can do what he loves best: talk and drive fast.

° A Crash Course in Being (Selectively) Helpless °

A Southern Belle is smart and capable. She plans ahead; she's always prepared. But she's never intimidating, because some things she just can't do on her own. Men crave being needed, and if your mama didn't tell you that, you were not raised in the South.

Okay, yes, sometimes we get men to do things for us that we could do ourselves. Is my briefcase really so heavy that I can't tote it out to the car from the courtroom? Honey, there's nothing in there but a file folder and my BlackBerry, but I'm giving some nice male lawyer the opportunity to rescue a damsel in distress.

I've noticed that this concept is sometimes difficult for northern women to grasp, so here's a helpful three-step program.

1. Beginners: when someone offers help, accept. Yes, of course you can put your own carry-on bag in the over-

head compartment. But why should you when the sweet young man with the headphones offers to do it for you? Say yes, smile, thank him. There, that didn't hurt, did it? And he'll help you get it down, too.

2. Intermediates: ask for help when you need it. Start small; ask your boyfriend to help you hang a picture. Or how to choose a new phone. See? People like to be asked! If you're a nice lady—and I'm sure you are—people will be thrilled to do something for you. Anyway I already know you lend a helping hand wherever you can, so let karma, the universe, or whatever it is take care of you, okay?

3. Experts: assume help will arrive. Flat tire? Pull over to the curb, and don't sweat it. Can't figure out which wrench to buy at Home Depot? Or how to program your new DVR? This is what former boyfriends and other gentlemen are for. Believe me, the age of chivalry is not dead.

Desert Island Belle

Of course, help isn't always there when you want it. I believe in being prepared, so I've figured out what I would need if I ever got marooned on a desert island. I would have to have lip gloss, lotion, French milled soap, and perfume for sure. A Bible. A Swiss Army knife, with all the blades so I could cut and cook and clean and scale fish. Toothpaste and a toothbrush—no, actually, baking soda, which can also serve as deodorant. Since I'd probably be packing lightly for this occasion, it would be good to have something that does double duty. I'd need a mirror, of course, and a flashlight. I'd want to be able to make a fire. Those Boy Scouts are pretty darn handy: in fact, why not bring along an Eagle Scout? Nothing but the best for the Southern Belle.

° *The Working Southern Belle* °

Entering the working world can be a shock for many young people, especially if they've just spent four years at one of our fine American institutions of higher learning. A forty-hour workweek just takes up so much time!

But for the Southern Belle, the forty-hour week may be just the start, because the Belle aims high. She wants to be indispensable. So she is the first person to show up in the morning and the last to leave at night. She figures out how to work the coffee machine and the copy machine. She learns the filing system, the phone system, and everyone's name on the first day of work. She finishes projects minimally two days before the deadline and starts looking around to figure out the next thing to be done.

Maybe you thought I'd be talking about southern charm here, but the Belle's charm is secondary in a work setting. Of course she is courteous to everyone, but more than that, she is professional. She wants to be recognized for one thing: her work product. And as much as style and beauty are the hallmark of the Belle, they have no place in the office. Work is about work, and pretty girls are sometimes a distraction. You don't want to sit across the conference table from a young lady who is more interested in her manicure than she is in the matter at hand.

Sometimes I hear criticism of women in the business world, for instance that a certain CEO is frumpy or boring. This is the one setting where looking boring is a good thing. I don't want to see your multiple piercings; I don't want to see your tattoos; I don't want your eyelashes to jump out and bite me. In the work setting, whether she's a waitress or a doctor or a fashion model or selling cars, the Southern Belle is a worker first—and a Belle second.

° Money Matters °

It's true that a Southern Belle never talks about prices. She won't bring up what something costs, and she never does that thing I hear in the North sometimes of telling you how little she paid for something. Why would you brag about bargains?

But we do need to talk about money in general terms. Otherwise people are ill-advised about it, and that is not the way a Southern Belle operates. Yes, the Belle is known to act helpless from time to time but never when it comes to her finances. That is just foolish.

∞ Don't take on debt. I never spend what I can't pay back. Sure, I use a credit card—a woman needs an excellent credit rating on her own, independent of her husband and parents—but I pay it off every month. I even pay my electric bill in advance. I can't stand owing money.

∞ Live within your means. A lot of people are trying to be impressive by bragging about their cars and clothes and jewelry, but the Southern Belle does not operate that way. Being fabulous doesn't mean wearing designer clothes and bouncing checks. It means being calm, well-groomed, and knowing you can pay your bills and have some spare to share at the end of the month.

∞ Create a budget. Ten percent of what you earn comes off the top for savings. Or 10 percent for savings and 10 percent for tithing, if your religion encourages tithing, which mines does. Then come the next three essentials: your home, your car, and your insurance. People don't know when you're hungry, because they can't hear your stomach growling, but they definitely know when you're homeless.

∞ Buy a home as soon as you can. Regardless of the real estate market, you need to get on the real estate merry-go-round. Rent just goes into somebody else's pocket, but if you own real property, you get the tax advantages as well as the investment growth.

∞ Save. Louboutins today, or treasury bills tomorrow? Easy choice. Those red soles are not going to take care of you when you retire unless you are a stockholder.

Everybody Knows . . .
Fashions come and fashions go,
but real property is forever.

° *The Belle's Morning Routine* °

Say you need to be in your car with the motor running at 8:30 a.m. to make it to the office by 9 a.m. Some women in other parts of the country might think setting the alarm for eight would give them plenty of time to have a healthy breakfast and get dressed for work. That would never be adequate in the South. Sorry! You'll need a full two hours to make yourself presentable, though you could shorten that a little bit by planning ahead. And no, it's not that Belles are short on sleep. We take good care of ourselves, and we know that we're much nicer after those eight hours. It's the late-night TV we're prepared to skip.

Here's what the Belle's morning routine looks like.

6:30 alarm. Feet hit the floor after no more than one five-
    minute snooze button.
6:35–7:05 basic grooming. Sounds like too much time
    allotted for this? Then you probably aren't thoroughly

pampering your face, plucking stray hairs from your eyebrows, and exfoliating your elbows often enough.

7:05–7:30 hair and makeup. This would be for every day. (Add another half hour for evening makeup and hair. If you're in a hurry that eyeliner will jump all over the place.) If you have a hair thing—you need to curl it, you need to straighten it, you need to wash and blow it dry every day—add more time. You know how much.

7:30–7:45 dressing. Could be less if you can put your hands right away on exactly the right undergarments, panty hose with no runs or snags, and nothing needs to be ironed.

7:45–7:55 cushion of time. Notice your shoes are scuffed at the toes, go back upstairs to polish them; get shoe polish on your fingers, wash it off; decide that's just water on your skirt and it will dry while you eat breakfast. My point is, you need a cushion of time for the unexpected disaster.

7:55–8:15 breakfast. The Belle is not one to trot into the office with a to-go cup and a doughnut. Just thinking about all that powdered sugar dusting the lapel of a

> ### *Pearl of Wisdom*
>
> Lay out your clothes the night before and you can wake up twenty minutes later.

blazer makes me nervous. Sitting calmly at your own table with a nutritious meal will make the whole day better. There is science to back this up.

8:15–8:30 another margin for error. Misplaced keys, wrong file in the briefcase, suddenly discovered drooping hem, coffee spilled on white blouse, traffic.

This is why the Southern Belle arrives at her office looking fresh as a daisy, cheerful and ready to be productive from the moment she sits at her desk.

What's That?—Sunday Best

We believe that you save the best of whatever you have for Sunday morning. If you're going to wash your car weekly, it'll be to drive it to church. If you're going to have your hair braided, or your nails done, you do it on Saturday afternoon. You iron your children's clothes; you make sure you have new bills for the offering plate; you wear your best, most expensive perfume. And if you have one fabulous pair of shoes, you will wear them to church. It is the very least you can do for Jesus.

Everybody Knows . . .

Mama is always right.

° *Belonging* °

I often say that knowledge is power, but there is another side to the Southern Belle's success: networking. Only Belles don't think of it that way. They just naturally belong to things. And while we're all familiar with the work that men accomplish in business or through charity organizations like the Rotary club, I believe women are generally more gifted at connecting with people. Just look at all the book clubs out there, and imagine the decisions that get made while the ladies are supposed to be discussing Jane Austen. Not just decisions either: women together share information, form opinions, *change* opinions, strategize, take on tasks, and delegate them. We all may not be sitting around big ugly Formica boardroom tables, but we get things done. And the Belle, Ms. Efficiency in a pink tweed suit, builds a network of allies throughout her life.

Affiliation for us starts with religion. Most of us in the South are Christian, and we go to church. It's just a given: on Sunday morning, the whole family gets dressed up and hops into the car and spends the morning worshipping and visiting in the fellowship hall. Many megachurches have substantial catering operations, so you can dine following the service. Naturally churches have their share of eccentric people, maybe even more than the general population. I'm not saying everyone you know from church is going to be your best friend. But spiritual settings allow you to discuss the big issues and important values with people you trust—even if they are not people you socialize with. A Belle is popular, so she'll belong to lots of organizations as she grows up. If she's in the suburbs or a rural area, one of them might be 4-H, the youth development organization with agricultural roots. Beauty pageants are important (see "Little Teeny Miss Beauty Queen" on page 225), and when she gets into high school the Belle is a natural for the cheerleading squad. She learns early how to get along with other girls and get things done without a fuss. But as much as she loves performing, the Belle will not take to the stage: some of those theater people are just too peculiar, bless their hearts.

In college, it's all about the sororities. I went to a small women's college in Macon, Georgia, so we didn't have a Greek scene, but lots of my friends at the time—and friends I've made since—went Greek. At the big state schools in particular, a sorority gives you a comfortable social network that would be hard to build otherwise. And the sorority ties endure: lots of girls join the same sorority as their mother or sisters or aunts, sometimes going back several generations.

There's a pretty big difference between the traditionally black Greek organizations and the traditionally white ones, and there still isn't much crossover between them. We've come a long way in the South, but Greek life and the people who are drawn to it are basically conservative. One of the biggest differences on campus between black and white Greek organizations is the black tradition of stepping. It's a kind of ritualized cadence, and it promotes unity among the members. Each fraternity or sorority has its own special routines that correspond to the style and character of the organization. The traditionally white organizations don't have anything comparable.

Each chapter on each campus is different, of course, but the sororities still have their nationwide reputations. Among black women, the Alpha Kappa Alphas are the preppy, pretty girls: their colors are pink and green, and their jewel is the pearl, naturally. Their white counterparts might be the Phi Mu, who are usually the popular preppy girls on their campuses. Other famous Southern Belle sororities are the Delta Delta Deltas, Delta Sigma Thetas, and Alpha Delta Pi. Interestingly enough, both Phi Mu and Alpha Delta Pi originated from my alma mater, Wesleyan College.

From everything I hear, there's a lot of ritual and formality around the sorority life, and Southern Belles do love a good ritual—anything that lets them sing together and light candles and shed a tear or two. But it's the bonding and the lifelong ties that are really important here. You might easily be introduced at an out-of-town wedding as "a Tri-Delt from UGA," and suddenly you've got a whole bunch of new best friends. Your sorority network can last much longer than the four years of college, because the alumnae networks are so strong. Just imagine a national convention of AKAs—that's a lot of powerful women in one place, and they've all had a very similar experience. If you're a member of that group, you're never more than a couple of phone calls away from any kind of help you might want, whether it's legal advice or the name of a really good milliner.

There have always been Southern Belles who were powerful in their volunteer organizations. I belong to the Junior League of Atlanta, and believe me, most of our members could run Fortune 500 corporations without any strain. And sometimes it is a real relief to meet with a group of people who notice what you're wearing, don't flirt with you, and can talk recipes as well as balance sheets. Or balance sheets as well as recipes.

° *Romance and Beyond* °

Look, I'm an attorney. I know that people have sex outside of marriage. I have read about the hookup culture and known a few easy women. In Atlanta, strip clubs are almost as popular as (if not more popular than) Sunday church service.

That doesn't mean I like any of it.

Southern Belles enjoy sex, but we prefer not to see it dragged into every aspect of life. This is important stuff, ladies, and I think it's a huge mistake to cheapen it. We have a phrase in the South that doesn't mean quite what it sounds like: we sometimes call a woman or her behavior "common." I guess the idea used to come from the olden days when social divisions were really strict and lower-class people were supposedly more promiscuous. Obviously it doesn't mean that anymore: now it's simply promiscuous. And maybe a little bit cheap, too.

The Southern Belle is anything but common, no matter how you're using that word. We are flirts, yes. But we are very careful about how we bestow our favors. And we are careful about the *appearance* of how we bestow our favors. We usually dress modestly, but we also know how to be sexy in a classy way. Your clothes should always display your outlines but not the details.

Men will take you at your own valuation. If you are hard to get, if you hold out for commitment, they will see you for what you are—a rare prize. Let those other girls hook up with college boys or wake up in strange beds with no idea of how they got there. You're the woman who must be wooed. I'm not saying you can't have fun. I'm saying you're going to have more fun if you choose a partner who's going to treat you well. In every aspect.

I'm sure it won't surprise you to learn that I don't believe in playing around once you're in a relationship. It's hard enough to get along with someone on a day-to-day basis if you do trust him or her. Sexual fidelity is just fundamental to that kind of relationship. It's a question of maturity: can you—or your partner—turn away from an extracurricular temptation because you value your relationship more? I certainly do hope so.

Let me spell it out: men will try to get whatever they *can* get. Most of the time, there are very good reasons why that can't be you. And you know what? It's not a bad thing to be the woman who got away. That way there's a lingering mystique about you.

Everybody Knows . . .

There is no such thing as too

much attention to detail.

Southern Belle Code of Honor

Of course Southern Belles are irresistible. We are attractive, and we are flirts. But we know how to draw the line, too: basically, I don't want what belongs to somebody else. That's true whether it's a piece of pie or a husband. I want to go through life making friends, not enemies, so I am very careful with other women's men. I try not to be alone with them for very long. Unless it's someone I've known for years, I won't even have a long conversation with another woman's husband outside of her presence. I won't go alone in a car with him unless his wife has given her permission and blessings. And I won't be alone in the house with him unless he is incapacitated and heaven bound. It's just easier this way: I don't even want the *suspicion* of anything funny going on. I once met this woman from Detroit who just couldn't stop complimenting my husband and had the nerve to attempt to have a private conversation with him related to our company in an effort to sway him to work with her. Needless to say, that slick move was the end to our very new relationship.

When dealing with other people's men and spouses, perception is everything. So I always err on the side of caution. If someone's husband is the most beautiful masterpiece of a man I have ever seen, I don't compliment his looks. I might make a remark about his clothing, but I know that just as I can see, so can his wife. So if I think he looks nice I am sure that she thinks he looks great and doesn't need to hear my two cents to confirm her vision. If I come to a woman's house and she's not there but her husband is, I won't go inside. And there are some places in the South, like Louisiana, where if a woman catches you inside the house with her husband, your friendship with her is over and you might lose your front teeth.

We Belles aren't catty either. Spreading gossip gets you nowhere. As my mama says, "A dog that brings a bone will carry one back." In other words, if I will gossip *with* you, when you aren't around I will gossip *about* you. That person can never be trusted.

Sometimes, though, you do need to tell a friend something unpleasant. It's amazing how helpful the Golden Rule can be. Remember? Do unto others as you would have them do unto you? Wouldn't you want someone telling you there's spinach in your teeth? Or telling you the truth about that unflattering dress you just purchased?

The territory I won't touch is relationships. You can get into too much trouble that way. I never criticize another woman's man. It's a surefire way to lose a friend. Even after they break up, you need to mind your tongue, because she may harbor a soft spot for him, and even if she doesn't, respect what they used to have. There are plenty of ways to stay supportive without saying a single negative thing about another human being.

But let's say you find out a woman's husband has been seen with other ladies. What does the Southern Belle do then? Well, have you seen this yourself? If not, you have no business spreading gossip. If you have, rather than go carrying tales to your friend, it's probably more effective to make sure the man knows he's been seen before running your mouth to his partner. That other lady could have been a business associate or a relative. If you didn't see them embracing, kissing, or holding hands, give him or her the benefit of the doubt. Still suspicious? Since you're a Belle, you can be clever about getting to the bottom of it. Just go right up to him with a big hello, ask him to introduce you to the woman in question, and mention that his wife and you are longtime friends. And as you leave, say with a big smile, "Be sure to tell your beautiful wife I was asking about her. Where is she tonight, anyway? With those darling babies, I bet." You've just told him that he's busted—and told the woman if she didn't know that he's married and has a family. Well done!

° Faux Pas? °

Do you know what "faux pas" means? It's French for "false step," and we all make these mistakes sometimes. It just isn't possible to get through life without occasionally saying or doing the wrong thing.

You are bound to make a faux pas once in a while. Maybe your opinion offends someone, or you're misinformed about cultural expectations. Maybe you just had a bad day and ran your mouth when you shouldn't have. It's not the end of the world, but you need to take a few steps to make things right.

∞ Own your error. Don't pretend you didn't do it or didn't say it, whatever you did that offends. That will simply keep the fuss going on forever. But if you take responsibility, it disarms people.

∞ Apologize. Just come out and genuinely say, "I'm sorry." Don't even try to excuse yourself or explain. It's even better if you can accompany your apology

Take It from Me

The first time I was in Africa, I was lucky enough to meet an actual king. He was sitting up on a pillow with his feet not touching the ground because he was so grand. I went up and shook his hand, which it turned out was absolutely wrong for any woman to do. Well, he did the truly polite thing, which was to put me at ease—he laughed and shook my hand and told me he attended school in New York and he knew what to expect from American women. He said we are all much more liberated than tribal women and he thought it was refreshing.

I was grateful that he reacted so kindly, because there just was no way I could have researched that. It was a real faux pas. But once you know better, you do better, and I will never make that mistake again. Nobody knows everything, and if you think you do please make sure to rename yourself "Queen Perfect."

with a wonderful floral bouquet or a treat of some kind. I offended the mother of one of my best friends once by booking some exotic entertainment at this friend's birthday party. My friend loved the anatomically exceptional dancer, but her mother was livid. Following the party my friend received a severe tongue-lashing from her mother for my gift. When she told me about their very caustic conversation, I knew I was to blame and not her. In an effort to make things right, I not only apologized but also baked an old-fashioned southern pound cake with cream cheese icing and took it over to my friend's store. I have to say it wasn't my prettiest cake ever, because it was a little bit lopsided, but it was home-made. And when someone goes to an effort like that and sincerely apologizes for an error, it's really hard to stay mad.

∞ Move on. Then you're done. You've made your mistake and made your amends. By handling your error openly you take the sting out of it and everybody can move on. Who knows, you may even be able to laugh about it someday.

° *Marriage Counseling* °

You can be a Southern Belle whether or not you are married. I know plenty of Belles who are single, widowed, divorced, remarried. I would never judge someone based on her circumstances, because anytime you try to get two people to live together, honey, you are looking at a whole lot of variables. And a lot of work. I do believe in marriage. I think it's the firmest alliance there is. But every Southern Belle is smart enough to know that not every day is going to be rosy. And that you have to work really hard to make your marriage successful.

It is so important to choose the right man. I do understand that this is an emotional thing, but women make such avoidable mistakes sometimes. Like the "dangerous" boyfriend who's full of charm but who urges you into behavior you will regret. I don't know how you fall for that, but women do it, again and again. If you have good friends, they'll tell you he does not have good intentions, but sometimes we're in no state to listen to wisdom. We think we can change someone, when the best we can really do is alter their behavior momentarily.

Good husband material for the Southern Belle is a man who understands commitment. That's why I say a man over forty who doesn't have children is a poor prospect. He's already set in his ways, and you can't teach an old dog new tricks. It would be much better to marry a young man whom you can train. I have always said that I would rather be a babysitter than a geriatric nurse.

He has to be smart and to have a good work ethic. He doesn't have to be conventionally handsome, because once the Belle takes him in hand, he'll clean up just fine. The important thing is, he must adore you, maybe even more than you adore him. He must have your best interests at heart. He must respect and understand your upbringing and be able to have an amicable relationship with your family. And the two of you must be in agreement about standards and morals.

Other than that, I wouldn't rule out any man as husband material. The Belle can marry a much younger man, she can marry out of her race, out of her nationality. She can marry out of her religion as long as there's some underlying spiritual compatibility and a mutual respect and agreement on what religious teachings your children will adhere to. Marriage is about what a couple can build together in the long run: a family, maybe a business, a home, some kind of charitable legacy, a network of friends.

The Belle always goes into marriage with the intention of permanence. She believes in "till death do us part." There are far too many ten-minute marriages these days, and I can only wonder what those people are all thinking. They seem ready to jump ship the minute they get bored or inconvenienced. Marriage is no picnic, especially in the first year. And once you have children, you'd better be pretty solid together, because that addition is like a tornado in the spring—fast moving and destructive if you are not prepared.

Playing around is not an option. There's an idea in our culture that you should be able to scratch any itch, but that's shortsighted. The Southern Belle is always taking the long view, and infidelity can only provide short-term satisfaction. The Belle respects her husband, and she insists that other men respect him, too. The allegiance of marriage is so much bigger than just sex. I would be more concerned about an emotional affair than a sexual one: if it's an emotional thing there's some bonding, and that's unacceptable. I can't share my vittles with anyone, but it's more disconcerting if someone is confiding outside of marriage than if they had a brief sexual liaison.

> ### Pearl of Wisdom
>
> No matter how mad you are, save it for later. My mama once told me the only thing a marriage can't survive is public humiliation and embarrassment— anything else can be resolved.

What comes pretty naturally to the Belle is expressing appreciation of her man. I'm not sure the ladies outside of the South are quite as practiced at this, but it sure is a good habit to acquire. If he looks good, tell him so! If he did something well, make sure he knows it. Show up for his special moments, like his office holiday party. And if you've got a bone to pick with him, don't ever do that in public.

Always stand by your husband. Lots of men have difficulty articulating how much the support of their wives matters, but I'm just starting to understand how important it is. Never let anyone tell you anything negative or damaging about your relationship or spouse.

Take It from Me

I recall an anonymous email I once received advising me that she saw my husband at a fine restaurant next to my office with a "young lady that was not as classy as me." I quickly had my staff reply to her, advising her that we appreciated her email but her assumptions were unwarranted and if she was looking for detective work that she should apply for a paid position with the local precinct. Then I called my husband, who had simply been meeting a client of mine to pick up a contract. I gently pointed out to Apollo that sometimes even meeting someone for ten minutes at a bar can be perceived as inappropriate, no matter how innocent it might be. The fact that this client was an exotic entertainer probably made the situation look much more exciting than it was! When you're married it's always better to err on the side of caution; unfortunately most people are more excited to deliver bad news and rumors than truth and praise.

Above all, the Belle can take the long view. She doesn't lose sight of her objective. I want Apollo and me to celebrate our fiftieth anniversary, so I try to overlook momentary annoyances. I know he does, too—he reminds me only once every week or so that my clothes and shoes take up all the space in our closets. I then remind him that his ATVs and motorcycles take up my space in the garage! Marriage is about compromising.

What Her Husband Doesn't Know

The Southern Belle has no dark secrets, but there are a few items she does not share with her man. After all, some illusions are important to quality of life.

∞ He doesn't know what her true hair color is, because the curtains always match the carpet.

∞ He doesn't know how often she waxes, or exactly what waxing entails.

∞ He doesn't know that she wears a girdle, though you'd think he might figure it out when they dance close.

∞ He doesn't know that she's had Botox in her armpits to get rid of the sweating.

∞ He doesn't know that she has her own credit card, her own savings account, and a safe-deposit box.

Dressing Your Man °

A true Southern Belle likes everything around her to be suit-
able and attractive. That includes her house and her car, even
her man. There's a fine line here, of course. You can get your
car detailed without any objections from the vehicle, but de-
tailing your man requires more tact. Unfortunately we can't
just drop our husbands off at the body shop and come back
later.

Still, this is the kind of challenge Southern Belles are
born for. We can recognize potential in a man and help him
achieve it without making him feel like anything less than a
hero.

The key is to think and talk positively. Say your husband
comes downstairs wearing a T-shirt that fits all wrong, is a
horrible color, and to top it all off, has some cheesy motto
across the chest. You look at him and flinch. Here's how this
conversation could go.

Southern Belle, in a disappointed voice: "Oh."

T-shirt Man: "What?"

SB: "Oh, nothing. I was just thinking about how much time you've been spending at the gym lately."

TM: "Oh. Really?"

SB: "Mmm-hmmm. Only that shirt, I don't know. I'm not sure it really flatters you."

TM: "Oh. I never thought of that."

SB: "Yes, I just don't think . . ." (She gets up and pulls at the back of his shirt, shakes her head.) "It doesn't really emphasize your shoulders the way that green shirt does."

SB goes back to whatever she was doing. This is important. She has sown a seed. She is not nagging. What man in the world isn't going to go upstairs now and put on the green T-shirt?

Take It from Me

Once a Southern Belle is in a position to go shopping with her man, she can make sure that no dud garments worm their way into his closet. The first time my husband, Apollo, and I went to a wedding together, I thought he should have a classy gray suit. Unlike most men, Apollo loves to shop. However, on this day he was not interested at all. But that worked to my benefit.

We looked along the rack, and I picked out one suit I didn't care for and one I did. He tried on the first one and came out of the dressing room to show me. I nodded and said, "Mmm-hmm. That's not too bad." It was a definitely lackluster response. Then he tried on a couple of his choices and I just didn't say anything. Anybody could tell they didn't work at all. Then he got to the suit I'd chosen for him. When he came out of the dressing room I was full of enthusiasm: "That one makes you look so handsome! Those trousers fit you like they were custom-made." By then, of course, he was desperate to get out of the store, and it was an easy sale. Did he know that I'd more or less fixed this situation to buy the suit I wanted for him? I don't think he gave it a second thought. The thing about men is, if you make things easy enough for them, they will do what you want.

Everybody Knows . . .

Those who know don't tell, and

those who tell don't know.

Breaking Up without Breaking Anything

Atlanta can often feel like a small town, but I am sure that even in New York, people feel that way, too. We keep running into people from our past, which is why the Southern Belle never burns bridges. If we break up with a man, we want it to be amicable.

I'm not a fan of drama. Every couple has its disagreements, but the Southern Belle doesn't pitch a hissy fit and run away from a relationship. There will be no shrieking, no throwing things, no storming out of a restaurant—especially if he drove you there. If you lose control like that, what's your next move? You can't creep back and pretend it never happened. And now your boyfriend thinks you're some kind of crazy woman. I'm not saying we don't have our emotions, but even when it comes to romance you have to think strategically. If a relationship isn't working for you anymore, you have to plan how to get out of it.

I'm no fan of living with a man before you marry him. A

woman loses too much control that way. If you already live to-gether, why should he make any more of a commitment? He's already got everything he wants. And if things go wrong, the Belle's options are limited. Have you ever tried to kick a man out of a place where he's comfortable? Let me tell you, it's not so easy to get him out of *his* lounge chair when it's parked in *your* living room.

Imagine this scenario instead. You stay in your home, where he may be invited to sleep over from time to time. All that boy stuff—the behavior and the paraphernalia—stays at his place. And if the relationship isn't going the way you like, you just get harder to reach. Say you hear a rumor he's been seen with another lady. (Only of course that would be a self-proclaimed "lady," because the real thing doesn't date unavailable men.) The Southern Belle always has a stable of suitors, men who would be delighted to take her out. This is the signal to move someone up from the second string to the first string. You don't have to confront your errant fellow—just give him a dose of his own medicine. And don't take his calls. Or don't return them quite as promptly. You can be kind and aloof at the same time.

This may go on for some time. Some men, when you get elusive, get more interested. They can't seem to figure out why you aren't head over heels in love with them. I had one fellow who, when I stopped taking his calls, jumped on a bike and rode fifteen miles to see me. My evasion made him very eager.

Other men will push for a confrontation. You don't have

to oblige them, though. The Southern Belle's line is, "Maybe we should both see other people. You're such a wonderful person, you deserve someone better than me. I can't give you what you want." Anything he throws at you, you agree with: "I know, it must be terrible that I don't like watching football with the guys." Or "You certainly deserve someone who is always available." Eventually *he* will suggest breaking up. And you can agree, with regret.

But that's not the end of it. You always keep a friendship because you might have to cross that bridge again, meaning you might need that relationship in the future. After a decent interval, maybe you'll reach out to this fellow with a friendly email, sending something he might like to read, or a comment on his Facebook page. I've kept in touch with all of my ex-boyfriends; I don't want to make an enemy, I want to make an ally. After all, I'm not very tall, and some day I might need someone to help me hang some curtains.

° *Good Housekeeping* °

I know with women's lib a lot of mothers stopped teaching their daughters how to take care of a house because they thought girls should have jobs just like boys. From what I can see, the only result is a lot of women who are, shall we say, domestically challenged and a lot of men still thinking that women should work, cook, and clean. Hooray for equality! Now I can only manage to get four hours of sleep a night.

In many modern households, women work full-time jobs and come home to dirty houses with a carryout bag of processed, unhealthy food. Many women never learned the art of cooking, and they don't have the first idea about how to make their families more comfortable. And it's not as if the men have those skills either. I know everyone's way too busy, but if you don't know how to boil an egg or mop a floor, that's a serious handicap, for a girl or a boy.

So I say, if you have children, get a little broom and a little set of pots and pans. Pull a stool up to the counter and let your youngster stir the cake batter. Let her or him flap a feather duster around and put the detergent in the washing machine. The worst thing you can do for your little Belle or her brother is to let them think that clothes get washed and folded by magic, that the pantry shelves restock themselves, and that to make dinner you make a phone call to some take-out joint. That is just not the southern way. And think of this—if you manage to raise a boy with household skills as well as the manners of the Southern Gentleman, the girls will line up to date him. My son, Ayden, has been helping me prep meals by getting the vegetables, cheese, and milk from the refrigerator since he was two years old. He also loves to clean up crumbs with his minibroom and dustpan, a true Renaissance Southern Gentleman-in-training.

° *Crafty* °

A nice lady from another part of the country recently confessed to me that she doesn't know how to do any crafts. In fact, she said, she gets all nervous and antsy in crafts stores, because they're so full of things she doesn't understand. I laughed like I thought she was joking, but really, I felt bad for her. Imagine not knowing how to make all those cute objects that brighten up lives in the South! I shudder to think what the inside of her house looks like.

It's not that I think everything needs to have sequins or feathers on it. But with a little bit of effort and some hot glue, you can transform the most mundane item into something really cute, and that's always a good idea where a Belle is concerned. Even functional things can be improved, the way fingernails look better with a coat of nail polish on them.

What's more, we Belles give a lot of gifts, and the best present is always personalized. I give a lot of photographs in customized picture frames, for example. Let's say I have a dozen women over for lunch—at some point I'll manage to get a flattering picture of each one of them. I'll have some standard-size frames and mats all ready, and I'll print the photos, frame them, and customize the mat or have it monogrammed with a design that reflects the colors in the picture.

I love scrapbooking, too. That's a big task, and I wouldn't do it for just anyone, but I love to put together scrapbooks and enhance photos so everyone looks almost perfect. (Maybe that's going over the top, but a Belle is a little bit prone to overthinking on the gifts.) Then I sort them all, place them on the pages, and decorate them. You can add appliqués and glitter glue and puffy paint—not all at once, of course.

Jewels are probably my downfall. I'll bedazzle almost anything: clothes, paper goods, camera cases, glasses, headphones. Everything can be made more beautiful and more personal with a little extra bling. Take a pair of reading glasses, just the ordinary dime-store kind. Get your glue gun out and put a little pattern of crystals along the earpieces, ending with an initial. Then you can stitch a little drawstring pouch to hold the glasses, maybe out of a remnant of velvet or really wide satin ribbon. Add your girlfriend's initial in a contrasting color. What a fabulous gift!

Of course if you have children, you're going to be doing crafts anyway. You have to have different colors of paper, crayons, paint, markers, fabric swatches, wallpaper samples, beads, sequins . . . there's no end to it! Say your little boy has a friend over to play. The children are finger painting. You take their little hands and cover them with a vibrant color of paint. Press them onto a sheet of nice white paper. When it's dry, you can cut the handprints to fit an inexpensive frame, write the child's name on it with the date, and send it home with him. It's just a simple gesture, really, but what mother wouldn't love to see that?

° *The Southern Belle Celebrity* °

We Southern Belles are famous all over the world. Put a girl in a delicate lace dress or a modern-day hoop skirt and give her a parasol, stick her under a magnolia tree or on a front porch, and you'll have the tourists lined up before you can say boo. And believe me, we do. Cities and towns all over the South have their annual pageants and parades and festivals. They bring in millions of tourist dollars to cities like New Orleans, Mobile, Memphis, and San Antonio. And often the principal attraction is an array of beautiful young Southern Belles.

The girls are chosen in a variety of different ways. Some of the New Orleans' private social clubs (also referred to as krewes) that organize Mardi Gras are open only to the descendants of the original families, but the Azalea Trail Maids from Mobile, Alabama, come from every high school in the city. What these pageants usually have in common is that the girls are between eighteen and twenty-one and are unmarried. (That's the official part: unofficially, you will never see an unattractive young lady among them.) Being selected is a huge honor, and it's naturally very competitive.

So what do these Belles actually do once they're chosen to be Cotton Queens or Fiesta Duchesses or Princesses of the Azalea Ball?

They do what Southern Belles do, only with a lot of eyes watching. They dress up, for one thing: most of the pageants require them to wear special custom-made dresses. The Azalea Trail Maids, for instance, get dolled up in pastel-colored gowns featuring full skirts, off-the-shoulder necklines, parasols, pantalettes, and fingerless lace gloves. Each dress uses more than a hundred yards of fabric and more than three hundred yards of ribbon. In San Antonio, the Queen of the Wondrous Metropolis and her court wear dresses with trains so heavily beaded they can barely walk. They have titles like Duchess of Alluring Style and Duchess of Venerated Temples. (I think I'd prefer Alluring Style, but they didn't invite me.) Sometimes this royalty is handed down in families: a queen of the Natchez, Mississippi, Pilgrimage might be the daughter of a previous queen and a descendant of New Orleans Mardi Gras royalty.

These mega-Belles have to be ladies; most of the organizations are really strict about upright moral behavior. No smoking, no drinking, no hanky-panky. They must be charming, since they will meet so many people during their year's reign, and they will be representing their cities. They have to be poised and disciplined, always looking polished. Just try waving from a float covered with roses for a couple of hours, smiling the whole time! Honestly, only a Southern Belle could manage that.

Look Pretty

Everybody Knows . . .
The Southern Belle loves her
three P's: pearls,
panty hose, and pumps.

° *How to Look Pretty* °

Southern Belles don't look "interesting," and not many of them are actually "beautiful" (though of course we have our share). They certainly aren't always fashionable, not in the sense of wearing the latest thing on the runway. But if you run into a Southern Belle's bedroom in the middle of the night yelling "Fire!" you will find her in a delicate lace night-gown with clean hair and well-brushed teeth and maybe a satin sleep mask. There will be no saggy T-shirts and ratty ponytails and dingy socks, even in the deepest privacy of her own home. She looks pretty, even asleep.

Now you may have noticed that I do not mention any-body's features here. Well, none of us can help the faces we were born with. You could possibly hate that little button nose of yours, but that's not the issue. For the Southern Belle, looking pretty is more a matter of overall presentation.

For one thing, the Belle is feminine. Personally, I prefer skirts and dresses over pants. However, high-waisted pants and pants with visible hem cuffs are quite elegant and ladylike. I love lace, beautiful delicate fabrics, and clothes with custom details—double stitching, embellished buttons, and French cuffs. Minimalism and menswear looks are just puzzling and not appealing to a Belle.

We're conservative, too. There are clothes in my closet that I bought as a law student, and I still wear them. You'll never see me jumping on this season's trend unless it's something flattering that I would wear anyway. We also avoid the extremes of any fashion. Our minis will be a little bit longer, our enormous handbags a little bit smaller. The Belle who follows a trend to the maximum extent is moving out of Belle territory.

Of course, anybody can put on a pretty pleated chiffon dress once in a while and that doesn't make her a Southern Belle. The point is that Belles are always consistent. Day and night, year in and year out, this is how they look. It's not a costume, it's a lifestyle. And it's not just the clothes, it's head to toe. The Belle's grooming is as painstaking as her outfit, also feminine and conservative. Okay, maybe we go a little bit wild with our nail colors from time to time, but we'll do nothing permanent that our mothers would disapprove of. Because you never know who you're going to run into and you don't want word getting back home: "I saw Kaitlin recently, and she looked a little bit out of sorts."

Everybody Knows . . .
You don't wear white
before Memorial Day or
after Labor Day.

° *Beauty and the Belle* °

I've never understood the appeal of the natural look. It's so easy to improve your appearance; why wouldn't you take advantage of the many beauty aids available to you? To be honest, I sometimes feel sorry for men, because all they can do to fix themselves up is get a new haircut or grow some facial hair. Meanwhile, we've got the whole ground floor of most department stores, just ready and waiting for our presence. What's more, there is so much research poured into beauty aids these days that for some women, I swear that time is actually going backward. And I don't mean that they've had plastic surgery. (Black women tend to be pretty reluctant to mess with their features, and besides, everybody knows black don't crack!) But there are so many antiaging lotions and potions that there's hardly any excuse for a wrinkle these days.

Lots of Southern Belles grow up watching their mothers' beauty routines, so this stuff comes naturally to them. But even if you like to think of yourself as a fresh-faced woman, free of artifice, I know it's my duty to tell you: you can do better. And you must. Every self-respecting Southern Belle gleams from head to toe.

The Southern Belle Beauty Basics

Hair

Maybe you've heard something about black women and their hair. It's a big deal. Even the most natural-looking African American woman has to make some kind of decision about her hair: will she braid it, crop it, straighten it, weave it, dye it, wear dreadlocks? For the Southern Belle, it doesn't matter so much what you do as long as you do *something*. The Belle's hair, whatever color she is, looks like she meant it to look that way. There will be no neglect, no just waiting to see what happens if you don't cut it. Nope: this is your crowning glory, darling.

Some styles are more Belle than others. We're not keen on the boyish, cropped do, as you can imagine. For one thing, you can't do that much with it. We love our accessories, and a headband or a jeweled comb just doesn't look as appealing on a pixie cut. We prefer hair to be off the face ("so I can see your pretty features," says Mama), so long bangs are frowned on. You shouldn't always have to be fussing with your hair to see out.

A neat shoulder-length cut or longer hair gives you more possibilities for updos and romantic curls, though childlike pigtails are not for adults. Wavy is nice; curly is fine; frizzy requires attention. Belles don't do frizz. That's what hot rollers, straightening irons, and serums are for.

Now, we don't discuss hair color in public, but that doesn't mean we don't think about it. But all we will ever do is try to help nature along. So a blonde might add a few highlights or a redhead could boost her color with lowlights. However, a Belle's hair is never a color that doesn't occur in nature: no blue, no red, or rainbow-color effects are worn by a true Belle. That's a whole different kind of look.

Skin

Is there a woman in America who doesn't know that the sun causes wrinkles? Quite a few, from what I see in airports. But the Belle got that message long ago. No deep tanning—it's better to look like a porcelain doll than an old weathered leather Coach bag. In fact, I think it's a woman's obligation to take care of her skin—it is the biggest organ in your body, you know. Just put yourself in the hands of some nice lady behind a cosmetics counter or a dermatologist and let her tell you what to do.

If you don't like a feature on your face, there are ways to camouflage it and make it look smaller or larger. For example, if your nose is your issue, contouring with makeup can give it the appearance of being more narrow or perky. While full, luscious lips are currently fashionable, not everyone was born with them. Plumping gloss and lip liner can boost what nature gave you.

I think a flawless complexion is most important. However, radiant skin that glows is usually more about what you put inside of your body than about what you cake on your face to cover it up. Want beautiful skin? Drink plenty of water, eat a healthy diet, and subscribe to a daily cleansing regimen for your skin type. Beyond that, makeup can make most anything else look pretty good with the proper application.

General Grooming

We're talking waxing, ladies. Mustaches and unibrows must be brought under control by professionals. So must those nanny-goat hairs some unfortunate women get on their chins. Nails fall into this category, too. Unless you are a professional potter (and I don't think Southern Belles generally are), your nails need to be clean and filed. I like them better natural length. I like color on them, too, and it's certainly all the rage, but to be honest the most conservative Belles are usually happy with a discreet American manicure or a neutral polish. And maybe plain red on the toes.

Makeup

We Belles wear it. We love it. It makes us look better. I don't even go downstairs in my own house without lip gloss and a smudge of eyeliner. There is nothing to be gained from having somebody—even your husband or your children—see you looking like a ghost. The art is applying makeup so it looks plausible. You don't want everybody squinting at your face, trying to figure what's you and what's artificial. I have certainly let myself be talked into some garish choices, like the crystals I wore on my eyes at my son Ayden's dedication. And I don't think eye shadow should match my clothes, especially if I'm wearing yellow.

So the Southern Belle will stick with the more natural-looking colors. The whole point is to emphasize your features and maybe smooth over what you're not so crazy about. Save the Cleopatra eyeliner for Halloween.

Everybody Knows . . .

You never put comfort

before beauty.

"Belle" Means "Beautiful," You Know

Being a Southern Belle has nothing to do with aesthetic perfection, shape, or size. It's a lifestyle focused on being consistently prepared and concerned with maintaining the highest standards of presentation. Whether you are short, tall, slim, curvy, or round you can be a Southern Belle. Everybody knows no one is happy with all of their physical attributes. Even the prettiest women don't like something about themselves.

As far as your body goes: no one has a perfect figure, but with the right clothes and shapewear most of us can look like tens! With the invention of body-lifting and -tucking compression undergarments, you can lose ten pounds in five minutes. If your bustline is the issue, you can maximize with add-a-size and cleavage-boosting bras (my favorite secret). On the other hand, if you're over-endowed, slim down the girls with a minimizer bra. If you've got gorgeous legs, wear fabulous shoes and beautiful sheer stockings. If your legs look like a road map of veins, take advantage of opaque stockings or hose with designs and strut your stuff like Tina Turner; no one will ever know. Whatever you love the most about your body, embrace it and don't let anyone discourage you from doing so.

I also believe in natural proportions. With plastic surgery every woman can have any kind of body she wants now, but if it doesn't look natural to you it won't look natural to anyone else. Ever since voluminous behinds became fashionable, I often see these lumpy, huge derrieres on women with legs as thin as a chicken's, and I think God would never put a rump roast on toothpicks, so why did you do that? Similarly double-F cups on a ninety-six-pound frame isn't a great idea either. I am not opposed to plastic surgery, but do your research and don't go overboard. If your essence is solely based on your outward appearance, please know that it is going to take more than a new set of breasts and buns to make you feel confident. The point is that there are as many great figures as there are women. The Belle takes care of herself, dresses carefully, and goes on her merry way, attracting admiring glances from men and women alike.

° The Perfect Fit °

I am always shocked when I leave the South and encounter the enormous number of women who don't seem to understand how their clothes should fit. Most of them are wearing their garments either too big or too small. I realize some women don't care about their appearance and can't be bothered to have a couple of darts put in a blouse. I can't do much for them—they obviously aren't Southern Belle material. But I suspect some ladies out there are simply unaware that they don't have to settle for clothes cut in a standard size.

The Southern Belle is never vulgar. She doesn't wear her clothes so snug she looks like a sausage. Even stretchy garments like leggings can be too tight, and anything that close-fitting really shouldn't be seen outside the gym without a shirt covering all the reproductive parts. But you know, wearing your clothes all baggy isn't attractive either. Some people appear to believe that they can hide figure flaws under a potato sack. This is such a misconception. We are women, and our bodies go in and out in curves, and what's more, men like them that way. Please trust me on this: sometimes tighter clothes are more flattering. The fabric should skim your body.

Of course we all have figure quirks that might require camouflage. I'm not a tall girl, so I can't wear a lot of the current cuts with a lot of extra fabric all drooping around. Some of us are as svelte as models, while other are curvier than a Coke bottle. No matter what type of figure you have, there is a perfect jean, pant, slack, and skirt that will accentuate your assets and hide your flaws. Looks and fashion should be determined by the setting, meaning at a business meeting it's always appropriate to opt for the "less is more rule." To spell it out, showing less usually leads to more success. However, when in a social setting and among friends, if you have it, tastefully flaunt it! Your clothes should always speak to your personal sense of style. On the whole, I think properly fit and moderately conservative clothes work best for every figure. You can always make them more contemporary with accessories in a trendy color or a fabulous bag.

Everybody Knows . . .
Northerners are fashionably
understated.

° That's Why They're Called Foundation Garments °

Here's a basic fact: your clothes won't fit you right if you don't have on the right underwear. Did you ever admire a woman's outfit as she walked past you, then realize her panties were showing through her dress as she moved? That's what I'm talking about.

This is a simple idea. Our clothes are supposed to cover our bodies and make the best of them. Weird lines and straps and bulges distract from that mission. But too many women seem to think that you buy a dress and pop it on over whatever you pull out of the delicates cycle of the washing machine. Or pop it on over nothing at all, which is much worse. My mother likes to say that there's way too much jiggling going on under that dress, and unless you work at a fast-food restaurant, you don't want anyone asking you, "Can I get some fries with that shake?"

Frankly I can't understand why you wouldn't have a

choice of garments in your drawers. You don't wear the same shoes for playing tennis and dancing, do you? So the bra you wear under a clingy sweater is not necessarily the one you wear with a business suit, and certainly not the one you wear for kickboxing. Some bras flatten, some hoist your assets out front or create cleavage out of almost nothing. It's worth going to a specialist lingerie store once in a while to try on different styles of bras. Most of us are wearing the wrong bra size anyway, and a good fitter can set you straight right away.

I think underwear should be invisible. If you're going to wear a pair of snug trousers, you don't want to show off a visible panty line. While sheer fabrics are all the rage right now, wearing skin-tone body-hugging body suits under them gives the look of nudity without you actually showing the world your nipples. If you want to wear a lace shirt, you really have to wear a skin-tone camisole and bra so people can focus on the lace and not on your underwear. I've seen runway shots of women wearing just a bra under a sheer top, but I hope that look stays on the runway and doesn't make it to Atlanta. What I am seeing a lot of, though, is bra straps—the back strap, too, not just the shoulders—as part of everyday wear. That is just tacky and cheap-looking. Even worse, sometimes it all looks sort of dingy, so if you must follow this trend make sure your whites are white rather than gray and your nude is nude and not dark brown.

Shapewear

I hope you think that every Southern Belle has a naturally perfect figure. That's certainly the impression we want to give. But because we're friends, I'll let you in on a little secret: you don't have to achieve this all on your own. Let compression fabrics come to the rescue!

Shapewear is available for every figure flaw and every skin tone. It comes in different strengths, depending on how much help you think you need, but I have to warn you that the high-power garments are not comfortable for very long. Still, we Belles know that beauty knows no pain. And there's no security like knowing your booty looks good from behind!

Outer Garment	Desired Effect	Shapewear
snug trousers	no panty line	thong
knit skirt	smooth contours	compression panty
T-shirt	no visible nipples	seamless bra
tailored top	no upper tummy bulge	camisole with Lycra
scoop-neck top	cleavage	push-up bra
sweater dress	all-over shaping	shaping slip

Take my word for it, if you want men to take you seriously, you do not want to be distracting them with flashes of your undergarments. And if you want them to find you attractive, should your lingerie have the starring role? It's the body underneath that should be getting the attention.

What's That?—Double-Sided Tape

Can there really be women in the world who haven't been introduced to this product? Ladies, I just made your lives so much better. There's a version you can buy at an office supplies store and of course it's useful for paper crafts. But there's a slightly stronger product with glue that doesn't wreck your skin. Have you ever wondered how models could wear plunging necklines without revealing every inch of their breasts? This is the answer. You just tape your dress to your body. Same with straps that are forever slipping off your shoulders, or hems that ride up. If in doubt, tape it on.

Everybody Knows . . .

Show your legs or your bust,

but never both.

° Dress Code °

"Knowledge is power"—that's my motto. So I'm always pleased to get an invitation that spells out what I should wear to a party. Well, not always: there's a new fad, especially for weddings, of getting a little too detailed. I've heard of wedding guests being required to wear a specific color or fabric, like white linen for a beach wedding. Not only is that too controlling, it suggests that the whole event is just being staged for the pictures anyway. Life is random and people express themselves in their clothes. You can't take that away from your guests. (Besides, I don't care for white linen, it wrinkles so badly and you end up looking like a ball of laundry in every photo.)

Here are some of the phrases you might see on an invitation. I don't know why it always says what the men are supposed to wear when it's really the women who have to make all the decisions. But I have never received an invitation that said "sequined cocktail dress" or "ladylike suit."

∞ White tie is the most formal, with men in tails and women in long dresses. Prance out with jewels everywhere.

∞ Black tie means tuxedos for men and cocktail dresses for women. Glittery fabrics welcome.

∞ Suit and tie: for men, what it says. For women, cocktail dresses that are a little quieter. Leave the Swarovski-studded shoes at home.

∞ Casual. This is a trap. If you're going to an event that's formal enough to deserve a printed invitation, you may not wear sweats. And by the way, we'd rather be overdressed than underdressed in the South. So men should wear a collared shirt and designer jeans while the Belle should probably put in a call to the hostess: "Ashley, we are so excited about coming to your pool party on Thursday. I'm just wondering what you're planning to wear." "Casual" covers a lot of territory, but you sure don't want to be in cute little jeans if the hostess plans to rock palazzo pants.

What's That?—Prayer Cloth

There are a number of occasions in southern life when it's not appropriate for a woman to wear pants. But sometimes these days skirts are cut so short and so narrow that this creates an even bigger problem—if you're in a situation where pants are immodest, sitting down in a short skirt is certainly worse.

That's what a prayer cloth is for. It's a piece of fine fabric, usually linen or silk about the size of an ordinary place mat, edged in delicate lace. This isn't a store-bought item. You make it yourself, and if you are a more generously proportioned woman, your prayer cloth size should adapt to properly cover those ample thighs and kneecaps. Your prayer cloth is always neatly folded and discreetly placed in your purse. It is only revealed when you realize that there is a need for modesty—during church, at a funeral, or even a formal public event like a political inauguration—you discreetly place that prayer cloth over your knees and your thighs and whatever else might be under that skirt. It's a sign of respect to the dignified people you're around. You do not want any man's eyes straying from the serious business at hand and wondering about your business.

° Belles in Black °

I've talked often enough about how much I like color, and I wear it as much as I can. I just can't see why non-southern women are so drawn to dreary shades like gray and olive green that don't look feminine and don't flatter most skin tones. But even the Belle needs a few black pieces in her wardrobe.

The Suit

Looking the part is absolutely essential for the job seeker. In my law practice I often have to interview job candidates, and I can tell you, some of these ladies are eliminated the moment they cross the threshold. (Hint: animal prints do not belong in the courtroom. If there's any drama, it should come from the defendants.)

Of course, you don't have a lot of money when you're first entering the workforce, so you have to buy classic items that will last. Every woman's first purchase out of college should be a good black suit. Ideally, you'd be able to get trousers and a skirt to match the jacket, but we all know this isn't an ideal world, so if you need to choose between them, get a skirt. Yes, I guess it's boring—if boring means you can wear it every day with a different top or shoes.

Buy the best quality you can. I'm not much of a discount shopper anymore due to time constraints, but I admire women who can fight their way through T.J.Maxx, Saks OFF 5TH, Ross, or Neiman Marcus Last Call. I know you can find wonderful bargains as long as you are willing to hunt and rummage through mounds of clothes and racks. However, when on a discount scavenger hunt, keep your head and don't buy weird things just because they are so deeply discounted. (I don't actually hear much about this kind of thing because we Belles never discuss the prices we pay for our clothes.)

Take your new purchase to a tailor. Yes, it adds to the price, but having your suit fitted to your body is going to make it look a hundred times more expensive and you will always feel and look great in it. The jacket should show your shape but button without any gaps. The sleeves should reach your wrist and not your knuckles. The skirt should be hemmed right around the knee, or maybe a little above if you're young, you have great legs, and you promise always to wear panty hose.

Prepare to accessorize like mad. We Belles love accessories anyway, and with black you're usually going to want some color, whether it's a pretty silk tank or a cashmere sweater or a gorgeous scarf. With a good suit, you could even swap in some glitter or lace on top and you're set to go out to dinner. (I have a stunning feather and lace collar that instantly transforms any outfit into a statement.)

The Shoes

You know what I'm going to say, right? Simple black pumps with a comfortable heel. Someday, honey, you can flash those red soles on a pair of Louboutins if that's what winds your clock, but for now you'll get more mileage out of something more comfortable and modest. (Not to mention that if an assistant in my office showed up wearing high-end shoes, I'd wonder what other employment she'd found in her after-work hours.) They don't have to be boring—you might find a pair with a flirty bow or a cute heel shape. But they do have to be comfortable and conservative enough for even the most formal situations. Don't go pining for those four-inch heels unless you can wear them for ten hours straight and put them right back on the next morning with a smile on your face.

The Little Black Dress

Once you've invested in your first solid work outfit, you can forge ahead to other wardrobe staples. Every woman needs a little black dress. After a black suit, it's the most versatile piece in your closet. I don't really like the way some women dress in black all the time, but I have to admit, it's practical. And if you can spend real money for a good high-end designer dress that fits perfectly, you'll be able to wear it for years.

Naturally that means it should be conservative. A sleeveless knee-length sheath dress with a pretty neckline in a substantial knit is about the most practical choice going. You can dress it up or down—why, you could wear that thing to work every day and nobody would know the difference. Monday, add a cardigan and sleek heel shoes. Tuesday, a blazer and boots. Wednesday, pop a long-sleeve shell under it and wear it as a jumper. You get my point.

Think of the little black dress as a canvas. You'll accessorize it the same way you do your suit. But what this dress does is go almost all the way to formal. Add some lace, add some sequins. Change handbags, heel height, stockings, jewelry. A pop of bright color in a scarf or a jacket will make everyone forget you're wearing your little black dress . . . again.

Everybody Knows . . .

It's better to be overdressed

than underdressed.

° *You Mean You Don't Have a . . .* °

I guess we all take it for granted that other people live the way we do, so I was astonished to find out that not every woman possesses a lint roller. Or a glue gun. Or a roll of double-sided tape, or a professional steamer. These are widely available commercial products, ladies, and they can improve your life, I promise.

∞ Set of hot rollers? You can't tell me you're just going out with your hair like that. Slow down, girl. Oh, all right, I suppose you can use the curling iron instead. Short hair? You still can use some sculpting gel and serum.

∞ Strapless bra? (Imagine a long silence here while I get over my shock.) Look, I don't hold with all this frank discussion of women's anatomy that you see on TV today, but I just have to ask what you are wearing under your strapless gowns.

∞ Full-length mirror? How do you check your hem? How do you completely assess your total look? And I do seriously hope every woman in the United States of America knows to hold up a big hand mirror and look at her rear view in her long mirror to see how she looks from behind. Go on and move around, bend over, check the angles. Think about it: you want to look good coming and going.

∞ Craft basket? How do you personalize things? At the very least the Southern Belle knows her way around the fabric paint and the hot glue and the iron-on transfers.

∞ Sewing kit? Well, what happens when you lose a button or your hem starts to come down? Sure, you could take that skirt or jacket to the tailor, but if you have a needle and a decent variety of thread colors you can put in a few stitches yourself in the time it would take you to get the car out of the garage.

I have even heard rumors that there are women who don't own irons, which I can't quite believe. The iron is a basic necessity; the steamer is the ultimate finishing tool. But I realize that some people just have other interests besides being appealing and attractive. So I guess we'll just let them wander around all creased and wrinkled, and we Southern Belles will look all the prettier by contrast.

° *The Belle at Home* °

The Southern Belle looks at her home as an extension of herself. That's why, even if she lives in a studio apartment, it's always spotless and ready for guests. What's more, it's pulled together, like the Belle herself. She's a handy creature, always ready to rehang some pictures or paint an accent wall. She loves her linens and her home accessories, such as pillows and throws. Her home is pretty and feminine like she is. Here are some essential features.

∞ A working kitchen. It's not a home if she can't cook.

∞ Seasonal decorations. My goodness, we love our holidays! If we've got room, we'll have entire sets of china for those special days, not to mention wreaths, centerpieces, and things to stick in our lawns. I have even known women who will put a Christmas wreath on their car (which I find very tacky).

∞ Plenty of mirrors. The Belle isn't vain, she knows mirrors add depth to any room, but if there's something about her appearance that needs fixing, she wants to know sooner than later.

∞ A way to hide the TV.

∞ Soft surfaces. One thing the Belle is not: hard-edged.

∞ Plenty of closet space, naturally.

∞ An ironing board, a vacuum cleaner, a dustpan, a wet mop, a broom, rubber gloves, a bucket, and cleaning materials for wood, tile, glass, marble, silver, and leather. Not to mention laundry detergent, fabric softener, spray starch, spot cleaner, shoe polish in three shades, suede spray . . . and so on.

° *Bad Slogans* °

Monograms are great. Sorority letters have their place. But for the Southern Belle, most other lettering on clothing or bodies is just plain wrong. (Yes, even "Mom" surrounded by a heart-shaped wreath of roses. Your mama would be much happier if you just spent that money on a good haircut.) I'd make an exception for a sweatshirt with a collegiate logo, but I don't really believe in advertising someone else's brand. If God wanted me to be a billboard he would have given me a flatter behind. However, I may change my mind if I ever launch a line of Phaedra Wear, but that isn't in the plan at the moment (see "What You Don't Know," page 7).

Still, enormous lettering promoting Mr. Ralph Lauren's attractive garments is nowhere near as bad as some of the sentiments I've seen. For instance:

∞ A tattoo on the knuckles of a job applicant that read: Boss Bitch

∞ A little girl's T-shirt that said: I'm Hot

∞ On a tight man's T-shirt, with arrows pointing to his biceps: Feel the Steel

∞ On a young woman's chest: I Don't Give a Damn 'Bout My Bad Reputation

∞ Chinese characters on your body when you only read English

∞ A baby's bib saying: I Poop on Demand

° *Bejeweled* °

A northern friend told me something shocking the other day. Her mother always said to her that when she got dressed up, she should look in the mirror and take one thing off: a scarf or a piece of jewelry or one item that would make her outfit more understated.

Well, honey, that is not the southern way. We are more likely to put one more thing *on*.

Here's the basic difference between the North and the South: up North they worry about looking like they've tried too hard. Down South, we want everyone to know that we've made an effort. And I don't know what's wrong with that. I think it's a compliment to everybody around you—you're taking trouble on their account.

If you asked me what my favorite accessory is, I'd have to say it was my wedding ring, and I bet most Belles would answer the same way. As much as we love all accessories, jewelry is special because it's often precious. Now, not only does a Southern Belle appreciate all the fine things in life like

14-karat gold and diamonds—she also cherishes the sentiments that get attached to them. So when you have an object that not only is a luxury item but also carries symbolic weight, well, that's going to be very important to you.

Our fondness for jewelry starts early. Some families have a tradition of a charm bracelet or an add-a-pearl or add-a-bead necklace. A little girl's parents will give her the bracelet with one charm, and charms are added to mark milestones. The add-a-bead or pearl necklace also starts with one pearl or gold bead on a special occasion. Then for every birthday or Christmas, her parents or grandparents or godmother gives her another pearl. They're not enormous, so the child can wear the necklace from the start, but it's usually planned so that when she's sixteen or eighteen or twenty-one, the necklace is complete. Every Southern Belle needs a string of pearls, and if you can't afford the real thing, you can just wear a string of good fake pearls until that changes. Most people can't tell the difference anyway. (I know some clever Belles who enjoy shopping for jewelry at consignment or vintage stores—small family

> ### *Pearl of Wisdom*
>
> Know how to tell if pearls are real? You rub them gently between your teeth and if they feel slightly grainy, they're genuine. I promise nobody will do this to you at a party, so you're safe with the synthetic version.

jewelers often have a selection of vintage pieces, too. This can be a great way to acquire high-quality gems for good prices. See page 166 for more on discount shopping.)

A good watch is essential, and I think this is an item you can't fake. You don't need one with diamonds all over it (though that sure is nice!), but a beautiful classic timepiece is an asset you'll rely on all your life.

You have to have your ears pierced, but only one hole in each ear. (And no Belle has piercings *anywhere* else—at least not ones I know about.) Every woman needs her diamond studs. I love diamonds; I'd have a diamond duvet if I could afford it. But let's be honest, diamonds aren't part of everyone's budget, so here's a piece of good news: your studs can absolutely be cubic zirconia. You get good CZs, cut well in a reasonable size, and set in real gold, and nobody is going to go peering at your earlobes with a magnifying glass, trying to figure out if they're genuine. They're so inexpensive that you might have a pair set in white gold and a pair in yellow. Because here's the thing: you have to choose.

The Southern Belle does not mix metals. I know there are watches and all kinds of contemporary jewelry out there that make this a look, but I think that's just a way to dress up silver and try to make it look more desirable. My serious jewelry is all platinum or white gold because I like the way it sets off diamonds, not to mention my skin. Precious jewels are something you wear all your life, so choose classic settings in the metal that suit your skin tone best.

It's not that Southern Belles never wear costume jewelry; we certainly do. Sometimes it's fun to mix the real and the faux, and something a little funky or ethnic may even be appropriate from time to time. If I were going out West, for example, I might wear some turquoise bracelets. Even down South, however, there's such a thing as going too far. I love my jewelry, but I do not want to look like a gypsy. (I don't want people to hear me clanking before I come into the room either.) It's easy to get carried away with big earrings and a statement necklace and pretty soon you barely see someone's face because she's morphed into a bejeweled mannequin. A Belle will never go for rawhide or macramé or anything that you could use to rope a cow. And she also knows when enough is enough. If you've got on a statement necklace, scale back on the earrings, and never wear more than two rings. The Belle does not wear 14-karat knuckle dusters.

And finally, if you're wearing a dress or a jacket that's embellished with sequins or stones, you're not going to put on competing jewelry, are you? Of course not; the Southern Belle is a lady, not a Christmas tree.

You Will Never Catch Me Wearing . . .

∞ those weird-looking orthopedic Birkenstocky shoes.

∞ all-over denim.

∞ anything without a waist.

∞ polar fleece.

∞ a naughty-nurse costume.

∞ those little reading glasses (half glasses) you look over the top of (there has to be a better way).

∞ harem pants.

∞ camouflage.

∞   a flannel nightgown.

∞   white panty hose.

∞   Daisy Duke shorts.

∞   footed pajamas.

What's in My Purse?

The Southern Belle believes in being prepared for anything. Spend a few days with her and you will be astonished at the various items she pulls out of her pocketbook. (Which, by the way, is always an elegant bag, not a backpack or a big sloppy nylon thing. You may wonder how we fit everything in there. It's Southern Belle magic, darling.)

I Can Always Find My . . .

Wallet
Brush
Comb
Full-size hand mirror
Cosmetic bag: one lipstick, two lip glosses, powder, liner
    pencil, eyelash glue, blush
Sunglasses
Business cards
Phone or two

Keys

Band-Aids

Double-sided tape (no wardrobe malfunctions, ever)

A sewing kit (ditto)

Pillbox: assortment of Advil, aspirin, antacid, and allergy
tablets. You never know who might need these, and a
Belle loves to help people feel better.

Breath mints (Belles do not chew gum!)

Clean handkerchief

Hand fan, the elegant way to stay cool

Pens that work

Small leather-bound notebook for jotting down inspirations

Little flat-heeled shoes in case I need a short break from my
stilettos

Feminine hygiene articles or reading glasses: Belles rarely
need both at the same time in their lives

Emergency hair kit: ponytail holder, bobby pins, and
decorative hair clasp

What's Not in My Purse

Any kind of contraband substance

Crumpled receipts

Used tissues

Crumbs

° *Mad for Monograms* °

I often carry designer bags that have notable prominent labels on them. But normally, I'd rather see my own initials on something I use or wear. I dearly love a monogram. What's more, there's nothing better for making a gift really personal than having someone's initials engraved or embroidered or painted on it. You could have a monogram on your stationery, your playing cards, your ice bucket, your suitcases, your cocktail napkins. I even have a monogrammed cake stand painted in decorative script. I admit I was surprised to find out you could get a monogram put on a hospital gown, but why shouldn't you? I guess if your ID bracelet falls off, the nurses still know who you are!

More Places for Monograms

Jewelry
Linens
Glassware

Flatware

Dog collar

Yoga mat

Umbrella

Shower curtains

Cutting boards

License tags, if you live in a state that only requires a single
    license plate

And of course a wedding and wedding registry are traditionally occasions to go wild with those initials. Back in the
day, brides collected linens and silver with their own initials
on them; they wouldn't add their husband's initial on anything purchased before the wedding day. But sometimes a
husband would give his wife a set of silver hairbrushes and
combs for a wedding present. You see them in antique stores
from time to time, with strange tools like shoehorns and button hooks and glove stretchers for a lady's new kid gloves.
Jewelers can buff out those old monograms and engrave new
ones for an entire new generation of Southern Belles.

I like monogramming for men's gifts, too. Belt buckles,
letter openers, handkerchiefs, a desk set, or a pair of cuff
links can be monogrammed. You could have a pair of heavy
crystal bar glasses monogrammed and package them with the
guy's favorite beverage. Men's shirts can have initials put on
them almost anywhere: the cuff, the chest, the sleeve, or on
the shirt front, about level with the heart. If you know the

kind of man who would wear smoking slippers—someone must do it if they keep selling them, right?—those could be marked with initials. I've even seen cars with a very discreet monogram on the driver's door, but you would need the right detail shop to pull that off.

° *Looking Like a Tramp* °

There, I came right out and said it. (I've been worrying about how to bring this up without offending my mother, who will certainly be reading this book to make sure I got everything right and didn't leave anything out.) However, some women look downright sleazy. A Southern Belle can be sexy, but it's always a discreet kind of sex appeal, and there are some looks you will never see her wearing. Such as:

∞ Tattoos: I don't paint slogans on my car or put graffiti on my house, so why should I tattoo my skin? Ink is permanent, and it doesn't get prettier with age. If you absolutely must disfigure yourself this way, make sure the tattoo is small, and get it in a place where it's never visible during business hours or with an evening dress. Have you ever seen a tattooed bride in a strapless gown? Nothing looks worse.

∞ Too much cleavage: We all want to make the most of our assets, but I've seen men actually be embarrassed by women showing too much breast. If there is any danger at all that your nipples will appear from any angle, you need to cover up. And that stretch of skin beneath the arm, on the outside of the breast? Unless you're under twenty-five and very slender, it should never see the light of day.

∞ Evening makeup during the day: You don't want to look like a vampire who somehow got confused about time zones.

∞ Short shorts: Some women should never wear these anyway, but they really only look good on the slim and young. At the beach. Or the track or the tennis court. Once you reach your thirties or become a mother, nobody needs to see your upper thighs besides your husband.

∞ Everything tight and short: If you have on a short tight skirt and tight shirt you are trying too hard. People will think you are desperate and seeking attention, which is never clever. Clothes should be balanced; if you are showing legs we don't need to see cleavage and vice versa. Unless you are selling what you're showing.

Everybody Knows . . .

No matter who the designer is, a

carryall that hangs from both your

shoulders is a backpack, not a purse.

° *Shhh . . . Discount Shopping* °

Since the Southern Belle never discusses the prices of things, I just assume most people pay full price for their lovely clothes and jewelry. I do know women who love to work for their purchases, though. They say it's like hunting, and as long as nobody gets hurt, I suppose it's a harmless hobby. I don't have the patience or the time to mess with the sale racks, with one exception: Black Friday. To get up and mingle with strangers at 2:00 a.m. searching for holiday bargains is an unbelievable rush. My sister, Keosha, has perfected this shopping extravaganza like no other. She can actually tell you two weeks in advance which stores have what, the hottest trends, and what time each item is available. Her ability to educate the salespeople on their store policies has made me aware of a few rules that make success easier.

∞ Never shop when you're hungry. Low blood sugar leads to bad decisions, in the department store as well as in the grocery store. Have emergency snacks such as dried fruit, nuts, or easily concealed crackers in your purse. (And if your purse is as large as mine, you can probably pack a three-course picnic without anyone noticing.)

∞ Ignore the discount. It's so easy to bring home bargains just because they're cheap. But nothing's cheap if you won't wear it, so leave those hot pink satin cigarette pants hanging there, please. (Unless you are six feet tall and weigh under a hundred pounds, that is.) And if you must buy everything you see, confirm the return policy and put all your shopping receipts in a designated bag for safekeeping.

∞ Fabric first. As you scan a rack of garments, only linger on the ones that are made of fabric you like. You'll be surprised how much time you save by flipping past all the blouses in beige and mustard snake-print polyester.

∞ Don't believe the size tags. Sometimes clothes are tagged incorrectly. Or the designer has some weird ideas about women's bodies. If you like something and it looks like it could fit, trust your judgment instead of that little piece of paper.

∞ Listen to the little warning voice in your head. Never convince yourself to buy a sale item. If you pay full price you can always bring it back, but markdowns aren't always returnable. If you catch yourself fidgeting with something, like trying to pull a jacket closed across your chest or twitch the hem of a blouse over your rear end, you won't be comfortable in it.

∞ Where will you wear it? Don't buy a velvet evening gown just in case you get invited to a ball or unless you can use the fabric to make curtains or throw pillows!

∞ What will you wear it with? Some garments need to be with their friends, like a pair of cute booties with some skinny jeans, or a silk shell with a cashmere cardigan, and that's fine if they will find a buddy in your closet. But some things are so bossy that you have to go out and buy something to wear with them. Say you get a really full brocade skirt. You'll need a snug top and very high heels to carry that off. If you don't have them, buying them just made that skirt less of a bargain.

∞ Do you already own it? That gray sweater dress might be adorable, but you don't need two.

Everybody Knows . . .

When you find panty hose you

like, buy six pairs at a time.

° *Dressing the Little Southern Belle* °

I saw a picture not long ago of some hippies or hipsters or whatever you call them from some remote city. The parents looked the way you'd expect them to look, a little bit bedraggled, but the worst thing was they had this adorable little baby all done up in a black onesie. And as far as I could tell, it wasn't even Halloween! The only excuse for putting a baby in black is if you're tacking a tail to her behind and she's costumed as a little black kitten. (Get your kohl soft-tip eyeliner pencil and draw three little whiskers on her cheeks, too: simply adorable!)

Little Southern Belles always look sweet and appropriately girlish. Their play clothes are neat and washable, in nice bright colors, and when they dress up for church, they wear pretty dresses with matching lace-trimmed baby-doll socks or lace stockings. What they *don't* do is dress like Lady Gaga in dresses made of butchers' best cuts of beef or Madonna with her pointy bustier. I'm honestly shocked by the way some mothers allow their little girls to get all sexy when they are just that: little girls!

Rules for Dressing a Little Southern Belle

1. No belly buttons showing. I keep hoping this trend will go away. I've seen enough tummy flesh in the last few years to give me nightmares. We wear clothes to cover our skin, ladies, can we just agree on this, please? And the same is true for your baby girls.

2. Save the sequins for Halloween. If someone calls your outfit flashy, that is not a compliment unless you earn your living after dark in a bar. This is even more true for a child.

3. No costumes outside the house. Of course every little girl loves to play dress-up. But I truly dislike seeing Snow White or a fairy princess trailing along behind her mother at the Piggly Wiggly.

4. No skimpy two-piece bathing suits (Brazilian bottoms) until she's old enough to spell it and know why women wear them, all right? I've seen padded swimsuit tops on little girls and that makes me ill. I can't understand why

a mother would push her child into sexual behavior or give a man a reason to look at her daughter in that light. Lord knows it's going to come soon enough.

I don't even like to see little girls dressed in the latest trends. Southern Belles stick with the classics. It's just practical to wear a lot of cotton in our hot climate, and high-quality clothes can be handed down to little sisters. Here are some of our favorite things.

∞ Smocked dresses.

∞ Twin-set sweaters.

∞ Box and inverted pleated skirts and dresses.

∞ Gingham, seersucker, linen, corduroy. All nice washable cottons.

∞ White ankle socks with Mary Janes.

∞ White gloves are okay on special occasions.

∞ Tasteful, conservative rickrack (if it looks Christmas treeish, *no,* ma'am!).

∞ Ribbon and monogram appliqués. I love personalized clothes.

∞ A nice pink or heather gray cardigan goes with everything.

Above all, we believe in color. I just hate to see a girl in black or brown; you know her mother picked that out because she was trying to be sophisticated, but those colors look harsh on young skin. Pink is the best color for a Southern Belle.

° *Prom Perfect* °

Some teenage girls see prom as the perfect opportunity to wear risqué clothing. Girls are often excited about their developing bodies and the idea of being women. They've got this great, new curvy body and they want to see what they can do with it. This is where good raising comes in: a Southern Belle's mother tells her over and over again not to advertise goods that aren't for sale. Attractive clothes leave something to the imagination. So the perfect prom dress might have a low-cut back, but the front covers the chest. Or the skirt could show some leg, but it sure wouldn't be a micromini.

Fabric matters, too. There's so much slinky jersey around now that clings like plastic wrap. The sad thing is that young girls are really the only ones who have the bodies for fabrics like that. But in the wrong

> ### *Pearl of Wisdom*
>
> If the dress requires exotic underpinnings or waxing, it is not appropriate for a teenager.

cut or color, it can still make them look like girls working in the wrong profession. And I know that young teens are desperate to start wearing black because they think it looks sophisticated, but to me it's just dismal. All-over sequins look old to me, too, though some sparkle is fine.

The perfect prom dress for a Southern Belle should be youthful, pretty, and ladylike. How about something in a charming floral print or a bright color? Spaghetti straps look great on teenage girls (and not so great after middle age). Layered chiffon is graceful and moves well on the dance floor, which you can't say about those tight bandage-wrap dresses. And of course, being a Belle, I'm never against a ruffle or two.

° Dressing Grandly °

Here's another way we're different in the South—we have a lot of respect for older women. I cringe when I go to California and see all those older women in skinny jeans and off-the-shoulder tops, trying to look like they're still thirty. I don't care how good your figure is, there comes a time when it's inappropriate to dress like a teenager. The upside is, as you mature, there are things you can grow into that look silly on a younger woman, such as a regal St. John suit. But believe me, there is nothing more elegant and sophisticated than seeing a mother in church on Sunday decked out in a wide-brim hat with her suit and pearls. No matter how you slice it, it says class, class, class!

For Belles of a Certain Age

∞ A good mink stole. We don't really need fur to keep us warm down South, but nothing is as flattering next to a woman's skin. When young women try to pull this off it looks like they are playing dress-up. Young bodies don't need mink-stole flattery.

∞ A high-end knit suit. They can hide any figure flaws, they pack without creases, and they never go out of style. But they can make a woman in her twenties look like she's in her fifties, so this is a fashion you need to grow into.

∞ A bold brooch. On a younger woman it makes you look like the kind of person who wanders around in downtown areas and follows her favorite bands. A brooch could be real diamonds and it would still look like something from a thrift store, unless the wearer is mature. Then it's a regal statement piece.

∞ A commanding hat. That is to say, a hat with a big brim and solid trimmings: broad ribbon, lace, jewels, a couple of flowers or feathers. Younger women can wear fascinators or those little bits of straw or felt tipped over the forehead. A hat you settle onto your head like a crown is a sign that you have reached the age of wisdom.

Have Fun

Everybody Knows . . .

You never get a second chance

at a first impression.

° *How to Have Fun* °

Maybe you thought I was getting a little too serious in the chapter about working hard. I hope I didn't discourage you. Because I'm not proposing you become a Southern Belle to improve the world or anything (though no doubt that would help). Southern Belles, ladies, get what they want from life. And we do it in our own inimitable style—we know how to have fun and to *never* have an off moment. Y'all might think you're tailgating when you stand around a hibachi in a freezing-cold parking lot in Wisconsin in December, but I know you know there's a better way.

Here's the thing: we are *sociable* down South. We love company. We enjoy visiting. We'll drive for hours to sit out on somebody's back porch and shoot the breeze. We tell stories and keep track of other people's lives, just like they keep track of ours. We live to celebrate the good things in life and that includes leaving it. Everyone should go to a good southern funeral at least once in their life, I think it would be an eye-opening experience for some people who have led sheltered lives.

The Belle also knows how to create an occasion. We love holidays, for instance. We'll celebrate every single one on the calendar, with new decorations and themed dishes and outfits. I'm barely finished with the Valentine's chocolate hearts before I start in on the Easter bunny and the lamb cake and the egg hunt. Food is absolutely central to this idea, and that's why I've included a few recipes (page 245). Every Southern Belle worth the name knows how to produce certain dishes, and it's never too late to add them to your repertoire.

If you are going to gather people together, you want to make them happy. That's the basic principle of Southern entertaining. If you look around your gathering and people are laughing or talking eagerly—or singing or dancing, which happens, too—you can be sure you are on the right path.

Everybody Knows . . .

Even if you know the truth, you

don't always have to tell it.

° The Gifted Hostess °

Southern hospitality is legendary for many reasons. Yes, we entertain often, and yes, our cuisine is special. But none of this would matter without the Southern Belle's skill as a hostess. She starts learning this as a little girl, when her friends come over to play. The principles are the same whether you're holding a tea party for dolls or a benefit for five hundred people.

The absolute first thing any hostess must do is make her guests feel welcome. I don't care how sophisticated you are, we all have a little anxiety when we step off our home turf. The southern hostess puts everyone at ease right away with a warm personal greeting and makes each guest understand that his or her presence is delightful. For a small gathering, she makes certain that she answers the door to her house; for a bigger party, she lingers at the entrance of the venue. She uses people's names, she compliments them, and she says, "I am so glad you are here." This is the make-or-break moment: if guests don't feel appreciated right from the beginning, they will not have a good time. Therefore, every guest at a Belle's party is made to feel as if he or she is the guest of honor.

What's That?—The Receiving Line

You don't see this as much anymore, but at formal and very traditional parties there is always a receiving line. A receiving line is when the host and hostess stand together in a central place and personally greet each guest with a hug or handshake as they arrive. This is mandatory for weddings, because all the guests are there to see and congratulate you. They call it a "receiving line" because the old concept was that a hostess "received" guests. If you've ever been to a big party and wandered around all night trying to find your hosts, you'll realize it makes sense. I believe the queen greets her guests this way at Buckingham Palace, and if it's good enough for Queen Elizabeth, it's good enough for me!

Everyone needs to be physically comfortable. That might seem obvious, but we've all been to parties that weren't thought through completely. Either there's too much sun or the air-conditioning is too cold or the noise is so loud you can't hear your neighbor. Nobody can have fun under those circumstances.

And you simply cannot invite a guest over without giving him something to eat and drink. What's more, everybody needs to know that you made an effort. If you're pouring punch into paper cups for a gaggle of seven-year-olds, put a sprig of mint in it. Lay out the cookies on a plate with a paper doily. Whatever you serve should be the best of its kind. We Belles are drawn to the more elaborate options, so if I have a tea party there will be six kinds of sandwiches and seven kinds of sweets, along with three different flavors of tea. But whatever your personal style is, your guests should never leave hungry or thirsty.

Guests should always know what to expect and when to expect it. If a meal will be served, if a speaker is appearing, if there's going to be a special activity, that should be obvious from the invitation. For cocktail parties and children's parties, it's normal to spell out when the party ends, too. Sometimes it's even useful to let guests know what they should wear, though the host should never be pushy about it (see "Dress Code" on page 138).

A good hostess circulates during a large party, and at a small party she's always paying attention to the dynamics of her guests. If someone looks lonely, she sweeps him up and introduces him to a handful of new people. Half-full glasses should be refilled promptly. Guests who have overindulged might need to be eased to a couch in the study and served some hot tea or coffee. The food on the buffet or the table should always be replenished and used dishes whisked away. Entertaining is a kind of theater, and the hostess is the producer, juggling the set, the action, the props, and the talent at all times to produce a wonderful performance.

Finally, saying good-bye is as important as greeting your guests. Well-brought-up southerners won't ever leave an event without thanking their hosts, so you should be visible as people begin to leave. I always like to send people home with a little party favor, but at the very least every guest should hear you say, "I am so glad you were able to come. It was wonderful to see you."

° *Perfect Party: A Southern Potluck* °

One thing we do a lot in the South is have potluck dinners; my family goes to one about once a month, but I know people who do it every weekend. Maybe this tradition comes from the days when people weren't as prosperous as they are now. I think it's hung on because it gives Southern Belles a chance to show off their famous cooking and social skills. Things do get a little competitive from time to time, but everybody benefits from that.

Of course you never arrive at any kind of party empty-handed, but if it's a potluck, you ask the hostess what she would like you to make. Maybe she'll assign you a dish that's become your signature, or suggest you bring a dessert or a salad. If you can't cook, you get assigned the paper goods or Coca-Cola (which in the South means any drink with carbonation), but all the glory goes to the cooks. Naturally you bring your best offering in an attractive serving dish so it can go right on the table, and if it's monogrammed everybody knows who gets the credit for it. People are always complimentary; you'll hear lots of gushing about every dish, even if it's nothing more elaborate than chips and dip. But the real compliment is when your food vanishes and people are asking if there is more.

Leftovers, if there are any, always stay with the hostess. Everybody knows you can't bring a peach pie and take half of it home; that looks awfully stingy and cheap. On a rare occasion, if you're with close friends, you might get sent home with a to-go plate.

My friends who have the best manners make sure the hostess doesn't get stuck with the cleanup. When the party starts to wind down, we swing into action and don't leave until every dish is washed, dried, put away, and the floors swept clean. It's the perfect opportunity to discuss the party, too, because the minute you start running the kitchen faucet, the men run away

Pearl of Wisdom

If the hostess happily packs up to-go plates, accept it with a smile and a cheery compliment. Otherwise, don't you dare ask for leftovers. The only exception to this rule is if you have the charm of a prince and face of a god like my husband—then you can shamelessly ask for leftovers and anything else you want and get it without a wince.

to go look at something in the yard. It's as if those cleaning products are kryptonite and the men will melt if they get a whiff of dish soap. Meanwhile we might just possibly discuss who's looking unnaturally refreshed (aka Botox alert) or came to the party with a store-bought cake. Poor thing.

Potlucks: Success Is in the Details

∞ Where: At home, at a park, at a hall, church, or community center.

∞ When: Weekend evening, usually early. Lots of my friends have children, and it's fun to get them all together. But they aren't all little Southern Belles or Gentlemen yet, so we try to get them home before they melt down.

∞ Invitations: Strictly verbal. The whole point is to entertain informally. But the hostess does need to give her guests time to produce a first-rate dish, so a week's notice is ideal.

∞ Decorations: Belles tend to have lots of china in formal, informal, and holiday patterns, often with serving pieces to match. For a casual potluck, cheerful ceramics are ideal, with a bright contrasting tablecloth and a couple of big bouquets of garden flowers.

Everybody Knows . . .

"Tea" is sweet and cold.

The unsweetened version

is "hot tea."

° Seating the Table °

We are famous for hospitality in the South. You can't set foot in a proper southern house without being offered something to eat and drink, and you'd better accept or we'll be offended. The only acceptable excuse is that you just had a six-course meal and you are as stuffed as a tick or you are feeling poorly and headed to the doctor. Either way you should accept our hospitality or give a very detailed and long, drawn-out excuse to make us feel better!

The Southern Belle dearly loves a theme party, but plain old vanilla dinner parties are important, too. And they are a great way to get the hang of entertaining, because the principles are the same, whether you're giving dinner for six or a charity ball for six hundred.

First, last, and always, you need to think about your guests. When you're putting together a small party, you have to consider how people will get along. It's a great thing to mix people up, but unless they have something important in common, you're going to spend the whole evening building conversational bridges. We Belles also do our research, so we know who used to date whom, who can't stand alumni of which university, who has strong political opinions he can't keep to himself, and who may have had a drink or two before he arrives.

Seating a table can be a challenge. Even if I'm only having two couples over for dinner, I like to write out place cards. It makes your guests feel really special to know that you thought about how they would get along with the people on either side.

Men should alternate with women, and spouses shouldn't sit side by side. Beyond that the hostess is free to do what she likes. Conversation is livelier if you scatter the outgoing guests around the table and put the good listeners in between. Sometimes we have to entertain guests who are difficult, shy, or quick to take offense. They'll need an extra dose of charm, possibly yours. Traditionally the seats next to the host or hostess are the most important, but sometimes if I know a guest needs extra help, I'll put him next to me.

° *Perfect Party: Tailgate* °

If you haven't been to a college football game in the South, it's hard to grasp how seriously we take this sport. Of course we follow the professional teams as well—after all, we have ten in the South, if you draw the borders wide and include Baltimore. But the college game gets people really excited. As you might expect, we are big on tradition, and families are loyal to the universities they attended. They start indoctrinating their children—including dressing them in team colors and teaching them fight songs—as infants. It's not at all unusual to have several generations with the same academic affiliation, so Saturday afternoons around the wide-screen TV can get pretty noisy.

But the real action is on campus, naturally. On any given Saturday, hundreds of thousands of football fans across the South load themselves into SUVs or minivans to make the trip to the big stadiums like Sanford Stadium at the University of Georgia in Athens, Georgia (which is my law school alma mater). They set off early in the morning and the car is packed tight with passengers, food, and drinks. I know people think they tailgate in other parts of the country, but until you have gone to a southern football game you do not know what that means. While I would never let anyone hear me say this and would deny it to my grave, Ole Miss has the most gracious surroundings, for sure, with ten acres of "the Grove" dedicated to red, white, and blue tents for really elegant picnics. White tablecloths and silver candelabra are standard. Not every tailgate is that formal, but this is the South—we aren't going to be happy with a grilled sausage and a can of beer.

Take It from Me

Sometimes I see pictures of women in store-bought football jerseys and I feel sorry. A store-bought jersey does nothing to flatter the feminine body. If you wear a jersey, minimally have the waistline tapered to accentuate your figure and add some custom touches, whether it be rhinestones or custom spinal tiebacks, so it has some shape to it. And if the colors aren't flattering, try accessorizing with jewelry, handkerchiefs, and hats. That might help.

Only a really unusual woman watches football alone, so whether you're at home or on campus, watching a college football game involves a party and showing your colors. The experienced Belle knows that she may need to do some re-search ahead of time. At some schools, like Vanderbilt, the stadium is full of men in jackets and ties and women wearing sundresses and pearls. The Belle seizes the opportunity to dress up rather than down. If team colors are the only way to go, you can probably get away with a cute sweater or scarf, maybe in the uniform's accent color. Unfortunately some shades—like the drab brown of the Texas Longhorns—are unflattering on almost every complexion. This is one occasion when flattery has to be overlooked.

Most women in the South have at least a basic familiar-ity with the game. We absorb it as we're growing up. A group of women gathered around the chip-and-dip plate probably won't be discussing the weaknesses in Alabama's secondary, for instance, but we can follow the action on the field. This is such an important part of the Belle culture that you might as well be able to follow what's going on. Naturally a Belle knows how much men enjoy telling her things, so she isn't shy about asking questions.

Basically each team is trying to get the ball through the tall H-shaped goalposts at the end of the field. The offense tries to throw, carry, or kick the ball down there; the defense tries to stop them. Each team gets four tries (or "downs") to move the ball ten yards, and if they can't do that, they turn it over to the other guys. The problem is that the ball can look awfully little from pretty much anywhere in the stands.

There's no shame in watching the video replay to see what really just happened. Keep an eye on the middle of the field at the start of each play. Some people complain about the stop-and-start pace of the game, but it's almost like a clean slate: if you missed the previous play, you get another chance.

A Few Classic Southern Rivalries

∞ The University of Georgia vs. the University of Florida

∞ Alabama vs. Auburn

∞ The University of Tennessee and the University of Kentucky used to play each other for an old orange-and-blue beer barrel. They don't do that anymore, but the blood banks in Nashville and Lexington, Kentucky, compete on game day to see who gets the most blood donated. It's called the Blue-Orange Crush.

∞ Clemson University and the University of South Carolina have a bitter rivalry that goes in a straight streak back to 1909, and lots of those games have been very close. Clemson usually wins, though.

∞ Auburn University and the University of Georgia are ancient enemies in the sport, with 115 games played. As of 2012, the Auburn Tigers lead the tally with fifty-four wins, but Georgia has won fifty-three times and they have eight ties. Now that's a heated competition!

∞ Georgia Tech and the University of Georgia have played each other more than a hundred times and call their rivalry "clean, old-fashioned hate."

∞ Louisiana State University (LSU) and the University of Arkansas have played each other fifty-five times, but since Arkansas became part of the Southeastern Conference in 1992, their rivalry has heated up. Now the schools play the day after Thanksgiving every year, and the winner gets to keep a trophy in the shape of the two states combined, which makes up what they call the Golden Boot. It's made of 24-karat gold—even a Southern Belle thinks that's worth fighting for!

Tailgates: Success Is in the Details

∞ Invitations: Send an invitation designed in ticket format, with directions to your parking spot. Be sure to specify kickoff time for both the tailgate and the game.

∞ Serve: Food for tailgates has to be durable and portable. Barbecue is traditional, and lots of groups have no problem setting up a grill and lighting a fire at 8:00 a.m. to be ready for lunch.

Southern standards: anything that can be grilled, fried chicken, pulled pork, shrimp, or gumbo from the Gulf states.

Side items: potato salad, coleslaw, baked beans, chips, nachos.

Theme foods: cookies shaped like footballs, deviled eggs decorated with strips of green pepper to make football "laces."

∞ Decorations: School colors all the way—banners, tablecloths, stadium cushions. Belles whose husbands have season tickets might even invest in matching linens and china.

° *The Southern Flirt* °

Yes, it's true. We women in the South do tend to flirt a lot. This seems to be very confusing to northern women. Maybe that's because up North everyone is direct, and things are more black-and-white. You're 100 percent professional, or 100 percent romantic, and there's never any possibility of even *pretending* to blur those borders.

Down South, we don't take everything so seriously. If I tell a colleague that he looks mighty fine in his seersucker suit, it's not an invitation. It's just a little compliment and a conversation starter. It's a game we all play.

But games have rules and some flirts go too far. There's a difference between "Oh, aren't you cute" and "What are you doing later tonight?" The Southern Belle does not get suggestive. If flirting makes anybody uncomfortable, it crosses the line. Then I think it becomes disrespectful.

And in the South, you don't ever flirt with anyone's husband, or in the presence of someone's significant other. In fact, we're careful not to spend much time one-on-one with men we're not married to or conducting business with. They can be your friends but only with their wives around. If I came into my kitchen and found another woman chatting with my husband, that would be awkward for all of us. But if we were all together at some formal dinner and she said, "Phaedra, I've seated your handsome husband next to me," that's all right. He gets the compliment, but she knows the rule is "look, don't touch."

° Make Me a Match °

No doubt about it, men love a Southern Belle. But a Belle isn't greedy. She knows that every man can't be hers. She is romantic, though; she wants everybody to be paired up happily. So, being a generous soul, she likes to make that happen. I'm very proud of having introduced three friends to their husbands. It's one of the nicest things you can do for a friend, isn't it? And I've set up a few more couples I have high hopes for.

You need to act with everyone's best interests at heart. I would never put people together frivolously, just to see what happened with them. And I think everyone should be happily married, so that's always my goal. But some people are confused about what they want and what they *think* they want. There are women who just want a man in their lives and they'll run after anyone with a penis. That'll get you nothing but heartache, I promise.

What's more, men aren't attracted to women who flirt shamelessly with anyone and everyone. A Southern Belle is always flirtatious, it's true, and maybe even something of a tease, but she's a lady. And in public, men want to be with women other men can respect. They like to think your intimate behavior is special for them. The Belle is a prize that not every man can win. That increases your value in their eyes.

A woman who's looking for a substantial relationship is willing to toss out the small fry. She'll never be rude to anyone, of course, but she's not going to chase after a man who isn't serious just for the sake of one night's fun. If you aren't prepared to spend an evening at home alone once in a while, you may not be ready to step up to a serious relationship. It takes work, you know. A woman has to figure out what she's really looking for. Otherwise it's like walking into the supermarket without a shopping list. You'll end up with all kinds of weird items in your cart and when you get home you still won't have anything for dinner.

Take It from Me

When I was single, I sat down and made a list of what I was looking for in a man. I wanted someone who was generous, affectionate, intelligent, reliable . . . and of course he had to be handsome, too. So when Apollo came along, I identified his potential right away. If I'm going to set up a girlfriend of mine, I need to know that she's at least partway down this road.

It's also important to really know the people you're matching up. First of all, do they both want to be in a relationship and not just some kind of hookup situation? I am not interested in just procuring sexual satisfaction for people—there are commercial arrangements for that. I also believe that the more people have in common, the better the chances are they'll hit it off. Do they have similar religious views, work ethics, tastes? And you can't overlook physical attraction either. Some men like big girls, and though a woman might have everything going for her, if she isn't big, it's not going to work.

Timing is important, too. You can put together the two most compatible people, but if they aren't ready to settle down, it won't happen. As people get older, things can sometimes move very fast. My law school housemate was a military guy, very quiet and conservative. He was really hardworking and he didn't get out much; he had grown out of the phase where you go out all the time and party, which makes it hard to meet new people beyond the pest control solicitors. So I introduced him to a friend who was a federal prosecutor: she is adorably cute, whip smart, and probably a little bit intimidating; she's a district attorney now. A woman like that is not every man's cup of tea, but she is definitely a prize. They hit it off instantly because the timing was right and I knew their personalities were compatible. They've been married now for a dozen or so years, and they have two beautiful daughters. Seeing that happen is a Southern Belle's dream.

° *Wedding Belles* °

I can understand how outsiders might think that being a Southern Belle is all about catching a man. And of course we Belles are irresistible. But I'm going to surprise you here—a Southern Belle wedding isn't a coronation. It's not just about a big fancy dress and a lot of champagne. It's also about your community and the way your role in it changes. And it's about your husband. Never forget the husband! I think some of those bridezillas certainly do.

I think having children before the nuptials is not the best idea. That's putting the cart before the horse. It creates legal and inheritance issues that easily could be avoided. However, things happen, so if by some misfortune you do have children before you're officially married, be sure to have them legally legitimized. (That's the attorney in me speaking.) The Southern Belle would never lose her head over something as fundamental as benefits to herself and her children. So the best-case scenario is like the old nursery rhyme: "Jack and Jill, sitting in the tree, K-I-S-S-I-N-G. First comes love, second comes marriage, then comes baby in the baby carriage."

It's always a good idea for the fiancé to make a special occasion out of asking for the blessing of the bride's parents. This is an occasion any Southern Belle would love. The bride should not be involved in the planning of this meeting. It is her suitor's opportunity to make a great impression on her parents— maybe a special brunch, or dinner in an elegant setting. This is an intimate and very important moment because there will usually be a very serious conversation following the asking.

The official engagement is up to the fiancé, of course. But the Belle needs to help out a little bit, in the background. She calls her jeweler ahead of time and says she thinks she's getting a proposal. (If she doesn't have a jeweler yet, she asks a Belle friend for a recommendation. That's what sisters are for.) She looks at rings and different settings and decides what shape and size best suits her finger and taste.

Here's where I might be out of step with some people. The ring is something people see, so it should be beautiful, but it's a *ring*. You can't live in it, you can't drive it; it's merely a symbol. You should be more concerned about where and how you will live as a couple than about a piece of jewelry. Marriage is forever, so you have your whole life to upgrade your wedding setting. Do not start your marriage in debt. No Southern Belle would do that. Money and sex are two of the biggest factors that lead couples to divorce. We know you can't always get everything all at once. Don't try to impress others and lose what matters the most—your spouse—because trust me, the same so-called friends who laughed with you at the wedding will be the same ones laughing at you when they hear you are in bankruptcy and/or divorce court.

I do think the ring needs to be a precious stone. We're not all diamond girls, but I'd rather see a smaller ruby or sapphire than a big chunk of quartz. It's the symbolism; this is the most important piece of jewelry you've ever been given. That's why I think it should be precious. Still, no Belle should ever worry about what her friends are going to say about her ring. I know there's a lot of measuring and chatter about karats among girlfriends. But the best attitude toward another girl's ring is, "If you like it, I love it." She has to wear it, not you!

Take It from Me

I'm not a big fan of the public proposal. What if somehow the woman has missed the signals and is surprised? You sure don't want to be popping that question if you aren't sure you'll get a positive answer. And fond as I am of rituals and formalities, I think an engagement is a pretty private moment. I sure wouldn't have wanted Apollo to propose to me via the Jumbotron at the ballpark.

There's a lot of drama these days surrounding the planning for the engagement. The Southern Gentleman—who is really the only worthy spouse for a Southern Belle—understands the need for romance and drama, so it's probably going to be a pretty special occasion.

Planning the wedding will obviously fall to the Belle, but the budget has to be decided between the couple. I really hate to see couples go into debt for one day's celebration. It's a terrible foundation for marriage, and let's be realistic, the first year is hard enough without adding money worries to it. Ideally, the two of you are setting out on something that will last for many years and include a lot of other celebrations. Blowing thousands of dollars for the opening ceremony seems foolish if you can't afford it.

Of course a Southern Belle loves a lavish celebration as much as the next person, and if there's an unlimited budget she certainly knows how to spend it on the most exquisite flowers, the best band, the most delectable food, and of course a stupendous wedding gown. But it's pretty clear that marital happiness doesn't depend on the price tag of any of these items, and we all know what's more important here.

Honestly? I think you can pare your costs almost to the bone if you need to. I feel pretty strongly about live music, but you can get a harpist for a reasonable fee and there's nothing classier. Rent a wedding gown—yes, you heard me. Rent. Why pay thousands of dollars for something you're going to wear once and clean for an exorbitant sum, and then it's going to sit in your closet for the rest of your life? You must have live flowers for your bouquet, even if you carry one single beautiful rose. But you *can* carry one single beautiful rose or a lily or a small posy of violets or whatever modest bouquet that makes you happy.

Take It from Me

That fantasy about your daughter wearing your wedding dress someday is just that: a fantasy. The styles will have changed, and she will want to pick out her own dress. I don't know a single woman who wore her mother's wedding gown when she got married.

Of course you have to have a reception, but the indispensable item there is the cake. The most expensive item is usually alcohol, and you can skip that entirely if it is out of your budget. If you really want to serve some libation, stick to champagne and possibly a specialty cocktail, which usually cuts the cost significantly. The guests who have your best interests at heart will know why you made this choice and they will applaud it. A nice fruit punch or tea flowing out of an ice sculpture or towering punch fountain always makes a stunning display. And if you can't afford a big venue, find a garden or local park with a beautiful canopy and call it a day. At the end, it's about the marriage and not the festivities. It's better to wait and have a fifth-anniversary celebration versus a huge wedding that puts the marriage in financial distress in the first year.

° *Name That Baby* °

I recently met a young lady named Cinnamon. This was in New York City, of course. In the South, we like a name to be a *name,* not something that comes out of a shaker at Starbucks. On the other hand, a lot of families are very keen on family history, and sometimes they're so eager to accent their genealogy that they'll give girls double names and then use them, like Mary Randolph or Susan Porter. That means you'll hear them calling out, "Susan Porter, come on inside now." Sometimes if it's the wrong combination, it sounds a bit like a law firm. The Southern Belle hits the happy medium.

A Southern Belle's name:

∞   is obviously feminine.

∞   is two syllables or more (names like Ann or Joan seem abrupt, like so many Yankees).

∞ is a real name, not a geographic feature like Sierra. And don't get me started on those people who name their daughters after the places where they were conceived or their favorite cars. I do not want to know about this. And if you love the car that much, just make it your wife's delivery gift and call it a day!

∞ means something. Preferably something nice. My own name means "Goddess of Light" or "shining brightly," and I try to live up to it.

Perfect Party: Sip 'n' See

The birth of a baby is a big deal in a southern family. Southern mamas think of their babies as little princes and princesses. Nothing is too good for the new addition to the family. The thing about the South is, everything is worth celebrating. And what could be more exciting than the birth of a baby? So we have the tradition of a "sip 'n' see," when everyone comes to meet the new baby. It's usually held a few weeks after the baby's birth. Guests bring the baby or parents a small gift or token, because everybody knows you never go anywhere empty-handed in the South! Unlike a baby shower, a sip 'n' see is a time to celebrate the actual birth of the new baby. This party is what it says: you come sip, eat a little something, and see the newborn. These parties are usually held in the afternoon. In an ideal world the new baby sleeps quietly the whole time while the guests take turns peeking at the cradle. But most of the guests are anxiously hoping that the baby will wake up so they can catch a glimpse of those beautiful bright eyes.

Of course, no off-color or rude comments are ever acceptable regarding the baby or its mother. Every baby is beautiful in the eyes of its parents, and every new mother is transitioning and adjusting to motherhood. No matter what a baby looks like, they are all special and the ultimate gift from God. Since a sip 'n' see is only for your closest family and friends, anyone who dares to act inappropriately should be immediately asked to leave and removed from any future guest lists.

Meanwhile, the new mom has a lot to prove. She's got to show that she's completely recovered from the pregnancy, that she is going to be a wonderful mother, and that her baby is like no other baby in the history of the universe. She can't say any of these things outright, but the message will be clear. Just check out what she's wearing: an adorable little dress, new of course, that shows she's got her figure back (even if she hasn't *really*; see page 135 on shapewear). Nails done, hair beautifully coiffed, nice neat heels. That precious newborn is also all dolled up for his or her first public appearance in a darling baptismal-style gown or beautiful lace pajamas.

A sip 'n' see is usually given by the new parents, with a family member or friend occasionally cohosting. Southern Belles love to organize any celebration, and a sip 'n' see is no different. As with any other event, custom invitations, catering, entertainment, and of course personalized party favors are in perfect order.

Sip 'n' Sees: Success Is in the Details

∞ When: Weekend afternoon.

∞ Where: At the new baby's home.

∞ Who: These parties are coed but limited to only
   close friends and relatives.

∞ Serve: Fruit punch, champagne, tea. Tiny cupcakes
   can be frosted in pink or blue. Tea sandwiches, cake
   pops, mini quiches.

∞ Decorations: Ornate picture frames with the baby's
   photo and family photo, ice sculptures, fruit sculptures, fresh flowers.

∞ Party favors: Any customized token that includes the baby's picture and date of birth and vital statistic information. Possible ideas: bookmarks, small keepsake containers, ornaments.

° Baby, Meet God; God, Meet Baby °

You might say that we're very ceremonial in the South; we have rituals for almost everything that many people don't even notice up North. And if there isn't an existing ritual we're more than happy to make one up, or to elaborate on a tradition that already exists. I suppose some people might think we sometimes go over the top, but we believe in celebrating the events of our lives. So naturally when we introduce a baby to its faith, that's a big deal. Some might consider it similar to to a sip 'n' see, except it's drenched in religion.

Depending on your denomination, the ceremony might be a blessing, baptism, dedication, or a christening. Parents often wait several months or even a year before planning this blessed ceremony, so the baby isn't still at that newborn stage when anything might set him or her off in uncontrollable crying. Depending on where and how you do it, it could be part of a church service, with a group of other families, or you could have your child baptized privately. The ceremony varies from one religion to the next, but there's probably water and definitely prayer involved. (The Jewish version of this is a bris, when male babies are ritually circumcised.)

The baby is adorned in white. You can still buy traditional long christening gowns with matching slips for babies, though some southern families hand these down through the generations. Toddlers can wear white versions of their normal clothes, a beautifully delicate dress for a girl and a nice classic shorts suit for a boy, with white socks and matching shoes. You usually have a couple of godparents, one of each gender. Their role is to take responsibility for the baby's spiritual well-being if anything happens to the birth family. Generally we try to choose close friends whom we know will take this responsibility seriously. Of course it's also good if we know they will actually bring a nice gift to the christening and remember their godchild's birthdays, too, but most important is that they will spend some time with the child.

During the ceremony the parents promise, on the baby's behalf, to raise him or her as part of the church community. The pastor accepts the baby into the church, then anoints him with holy oil or water, a little or a lot depending on your denomination. It doesn't usually take very long, though of course there's a homily or a sermon. And, because we are in the South, there will be a lovely reception afterward.

° *The Little Belle at Play* °

I guess we all know by now that children learn a lot about life by playing pretend. That's certainly true for the little Southern Belle. In fact, it's sometimes amazing how close her pretending comes to the actual life of a grown-up Belle. For instance, I started cooking with an Easy-Bake oven at six years old and I've never stopped baking since. Once you've whipped up a batch of cupcakes or cookies, the next step is obviously a tea party. The guests could be humans or they could be dolls. The dolls tend to be more cooperative, but a girl learns more about the challenges of entertaining from human beings. Those lessons about taking turns, sharing, and making people feel special can start with tiny teacups full of apple juice.

Naturally little Southern Belles want to emulate their mamas in every way, so playing "beauty shop" is also important. But those beauty experiments better not be permanent, so keep the real scissors out of sight. And no matter how glammed-up the girls get, every bit of makeup and nail polish comes off before they go home.

Maybe they'll want to play store, too—a toy cash register can provide hours of fun, especially if it's combined with a dress-up chest. (That's where all the Southern Belle mama's wardrobe mistakes go, along with old prom and bridesmaid dresses.) This is also where the focus on accessories starts. The finishing touches like gloves, pocketbooks, and fans really make an outfit, so girls learn early how to pull everything together. Pretend fashion shows are also popular, but never underwear or bathing suits: Southern Belle babies are not Victoria's Secret model material! They are age-appropriate southern angels in training waiting to earn their Belle wings.

Take It from Me

Playing pretend is an all-around plus, but I'm not so crazy about TV or video games. I want to be the source of information for my child. I don't want him learning all this nonsense from people who are just trying to sell him things. I don't want the TV to be the parent, I want that to be me or my husband, Apollo, or my parents. And pop culture is full of children behaving disrespectfully; I don't want Ayden thinking that's how children behave. Television often portrays children sassing their parents in a comedic light, but trust me, there is nothing funny or cute about a child talking back or being disrespectful to any adult. That's not good southern raising, and it won't happen in a Southern Belle's house.

° *Perfect Party: Princess* °

Most little girls in America probably want to be princesses at some point. I know I did, and it still seems to be part of the culture, because I see a lot of princess parties at local spas. I would have just loved this kind of party when I was a youngster! The girls come all dressed up in princess costumes with their little tiaras and they get the manicures and pedicures. Usually there is a fashion show and hors d'oeuvres and lunch or dinner fit for a princess.

Now this could obviously go all wrong, but I'm not talking about putting on stiletto nails or appliqués or any of that grown-up nonsense. And I don't like makeup on children. Lord, I spend half my life trying to make my skin look more like a child's!

A princess party is an exciting special treat. No Southern Belle is going to make weekly mani-pedi appointments for her grade-school daughter. But it is an introduction to the idea of maintaining your looks. What I really like about these parties—or any children's parties—is that they also help children learn how to be hostesses. A smart mother gets her daughter involved in planning the guest list: if Katie is included, will Kylie feel left out? Mother and daughter can put the gift bags together and greet their guests at the door of the spa, making each of them feel welcome. The mom should be helping her daughter think ahead: How can you make this little girl feel special? What's the best way to help all these personalities get along together? For the Southern Belle, entertaining is giving her guests an experience, and we start learning this skill early.

Princess Party: Success Is in the Details

∞ Invitations: A calligraphy scroll inviting each girl to attend court festivities at the spa.

∞ Transportation: Limousine service for all the guests.

∞ Menu: Punch or juice in plastic champagne glasses or goblets; petit fours or cupcakes frosted with fondant and accented with glitter sugar or edible "pearls" and the usual cheese straws, finger sandwiches, and of course fresh fruit skewers.

∞ Decorations: A red carpet, a throne for the birthday princess, and anything sparkling you can lay your hands on, as well as fresh flowers.

∞ Party favors: Tiaras, beaded jewelry, gift bags with tiny bottles of nail polish and flavored lip glosses.

° *Halloween Costumes* °

We Southern Belles love to entertain, and we love theme parties, so Halloween is a big deal for us. What's more, we don't like to go to Toys "R" Us to buy a child's costume: it just isn't very personal. And besides, we think TV characters are basically tacky.

Babies costumed as fruits and vegetables are adorable, and they're too little to complain as long as their pumpkin-stem or sunflower-blossom hats aren't uncomfortable. Toddlers make wonderful animals, since they're going to be wiggling around anyway. For the average person, just attaching a tail to some leggings and some ears to a headband is a good start on most animal costumes. But, for the Southern Belle, if you want to be a lion you have to really look the part: what is truly needed is a visit to the fabric store to buy a pattern and either making it yourself or finding someone who can make it perfectly.

Older girls, of course, want to be princesses or fairies, though we avoid the Disney versions if we can. A full skirt, some tulle, and a glittery tiara is pretty easy to put together. What the young Southern Belle does not do is wear her Halloween costume to school, to church, or to the supermarket. If she's lucky enough to be a Southern Belle, she doesn't need to dress up as anyone else, she is already a princess in her own right.

° Little Teeny Miss Beauty Queen °

Okay, don't get all worked up now. I know some people think it's a terrible thing to put your little girl in a beauty pageant, but pageantry is important in the South, and a lot of Southern Belles benefit from participating. I'm not just talking about the scholarships that some pageants offer as prizes. For most girls, whatever they win won't come close to paying for their entry fees or the cost of their hand-beaded gowns and talent costumes. But lots of southern parents think pageantry is worth it because nobody is as charming and poised as a southern beauty queen. And there are enough pageants, so eventually every girl—no matter *what* she looks like—will probably win something.

In a lot of rural places, this is just what you do with your girls and sometimes toddler boys. It's fun for them—the mamas fuss over them and dress them up like living dolls. They make friends on the pageant circuit, and the mamas get to know each other, too. Girls learn how to walk gracefully, how to smile like they mean it, and how to eloquently speak to strangers.

Come to think of it, pageantry may be one of the reasons I like fashion so much, because we got to wear the kinds of dresses little girls think are just wonderful, with sparkling beads and big, rustling hoop skirts. I probably did ten or fifteen of these pageants, but the first one I remember was at Mount Pleasant Baptist Church. I couldn't have been much more than five years old. There was a boys' pageant, too, and the winner of the girls' pageant "married" the little king, they called him. I remember it clear as day: I had a little white wedding dress with baby-doll white socks trimmed with lace and white patent-leather Mary Jane shoes. I guess my attraction to shoes goes way back! And I had a little bouquet with white roses and white gloves that went up my arms. My "groom" wore a little charcoal-gray tuxedo with one of the ruffled shirts that were so fashionable back then. Actually I "married" him twice, when I was five and when I was six! I'm glad it ended there because I don't think he was such a catch after he hit adolescence.

There are dozens of these pageants, and a lot of them are very local. You might be Junior Teen Miss Celery City (that's Sanford, Florida), or Alabama Forestry Petite Miss, or Wee Miss Pageland Watermelon (in South Carolina). Some of the pageants are classified as "natural," which means the competition is based on what they call "natural beauty" and personality. Other pageants go ahead and have those little girls all dolled up with full stage makeup and curled, teased hair and flippers, also known as kiddy veneers/dentures. You can probably tell by now that the Southern Belle's mama would prefer not to have her baby girl rush into that hair and makeup situation too early on, but she will compromise if that is all that is available.

A lot of these pageants are big community builders. All over the South we've got our local festivals and parades, and most of them feature a pretty girl with perfect hair, a rhinestone tiara, and a sash. She'll be smiling and waving, and if you meet her, she'll have something nice to say to you. Southern Belles have a lot in common with beauty queens: grooming, discipline, and, most of all, a friendly word for everyone they meet.

° *Dating in the Slow Lane* °

Everybody wants to date the Southern Belle, but here's the first thing boys have to learn: good things come to those who wait. No Belle worthy of the name is going to be ready for a real boyfriend before she reaches the age of fifteen or sixteen. At least, not according to her mama, and as you've no doubt figured out by now, Mama always knows best. A girl has the rest of her life to fascinate the opposite sex.

Take It from Me

My mama always used to say, "When you can't find a job, food, or a hot bath, you can find a man willing to have a tryst." Hence, know and understand that a lady's self-worth is located between her ears and not between her legs.

High school is a good time to concentrate on schoolwork and extracurricular activities that involve forming bonds with girls. Sure, every Belle has males wrapped around her little finger, but every Belle also knows it's women who matter on the social side of things.

Once a girl is old enough to start going around with boys, there are strict limits on whom she dates and what they do together. You think it's as simple as "Bobby and I are going to the movies"? No, indeed! And by the way, I might as well say right here that a Southern Belle is not going to be having sex with a high school boyfriend. It simply will not happen.

Take It from Me

As my mama used to say to me, "Why would anyone buy the cow if you give away the milk?" Even when they're teenagers, Southern Belles know they are worth waiting for.

And I have to put it bluntly: Belles don't date losers. Good grades, good manners, great potential, and a good haircut are the bare minimum requirements. Do you think a Southern Belle is going to ride in a car that has soda cans and

McDonald's wrappers on the floor? Maybe once, in an emergency, she might—but never twice.

If you take a Southern Belle out, she's not splitting the check either. (I say this for my readers up North, because I hear terrible stories about women expecting to pay for themselves on dates. That is just unacceptable.) If all a boy can afford is a milkshake, then he can take his young lady out for milkshakes.

A date with a Belle is no time for a boy to experiment with "alternative" clothes or grooming either. He'd better be neatly groomed and fashionably dressed. A young man can't go wrong with pressed slacks and a collared or polo shirt. Gym shorts and T-shirts are fine, too—but only if he plans to play basketball. A white T-shirt, visible underwear, and a baseball cap are never appropriate for a date.

The real test of a boy's worth is meeting a Belle's parents. You didn't think a good southern mama was going to let her daughter go out with just anyone, did you? A boy who knows what's good for him will expect to spend some time visiting with his little Belle's mama before they are permitted to leave the house. Of course Jennifer isn't ready. Even at a young age, the Belle understands the value of making an entrance. So young John has to sit with Mrs. Smith making small talk and hope she doesn't notice his sweaty palms. He had better say, "Hello, Mrs. Smith, I'm John Doe. It's so nice to meet you. I'm here to pick up Jennifer." Then he tells Mrs. Smith he sees exactly where Jennifer gets her good looks; it obviously runs in the family. He stands up when Jennifer comes into the room. He calls Mrs. Smith "ma'am." He shakes her hand again when he leaves and repeats how nice it was to meet her. He then opens the house door and car door for Jennifer, always allowing her to exit first. Even if it doesn't look like Mama is watching. (She's watching. Count on it.) Finally, he brings Jennifer home on time after every single date.

Everybody Knows . . .

You want to leave a man with a

few illusions about you.

° *The Southern Gentleman* °

Naturally the Southern Belle only dates men who are worthy of her and raises boys to be gentlemen, always demonstrating respect for women. I've heard that up North some men don't understand what's expected of them, so here's the list.

A Southern Gentleman Always . . .

∞ addresses a lady politely, whether she's "Mrs. Smith" or "Ms. Julia" or "Aunt Caroline." He doesn't jump to first names unless he is invited to or unless he and the lady in question are peers.

∞ keeps his language clean. I know there are four-letter words out there, but the Southern Belle and the people she travels with prefer to use more words rather than less. For instance, why say "liquor" when you can say "adult refreshment"? It creates a much better impression, and the Southern Gentleman is all about creating an impression.

∞ picks up every check. His reward is the pleasure of the Southern Belle's company. Period.

∞ brings gifts. Flowers, trinkets, jewelry. You could call this "tribute." We women deserve it, don't you think?

∞ opens every door, carries every package. Ooooh, honey, I am *helpless*! With my freshly manicured nails and my four-inch heels and snug little skirt, I can barely get from the front steps to the car. You can't be thinking I'm going to open that car door my-self, are you? Why, I don't think I know how.

Of course if nobody is around, the Belle can not only get herself into her car, she can probably change the spark plugs and the motor mounts, if needed. But nobody will ever see that happen and survive to tell about it. The fiction is that the lady must be sheltered, aided, and cherished. It's a little game we all play in the South.

° *How to Be a Grande Dame* °

I am really looking forward to this stage of life. In the South we have a little bit more respect for age than in some areas of the country; you'd never catch a southern woman trying to pass herself off as younger than she actually is. In our churches we often address the older ladies as "Mother." They have earned the right to their dignity and respect. When I get to be, oh, sixty-five or seventy, I am going to:

∞   let my hair go gray if it looks good on me.

∞   carry a beautiful custom cane, whether I need it or not. I can never have too many accessories.

∞   wear a big, beautiful hat whenever I go outdoors.

∞   eat whatever I want, whenever I want.

∞   let other people drive me around. Why worry about traffic?

∞ call everyone "dear." It puts them in their place.

∞ use a hand fan. A nice, big ornate one, not one of those little paper church fans.

∞ leave parties when I get bored.

∞ scare the stuffing out of young men.

∞ remember where all the bodies are buried.

And last but not least, when I am a grande dame, I will say what I want, when and how I want to!

° The Final Rest °

You can't discuss the life cycle of the Southern Belle without discussing funerals, because in the South the way we leave life is very, very important. As a mortician-in-training I probably pay closer attention to this than most people, and in the black community we just love a good funeral. It is one of the most important events in our lives. You've heard the saying "Less is more"? That is not true in my world when it comes to burying a loved one.

A lot depends on finding a good funeral home. Many of them are still family businesses that have dealt with the same customers for several generations. They are also still racially divided; there are black funeral homes and white funeral homes, and we don't normally bury each other's people. That may have something to do with our churches—Sunday morning in the South is still pretty segregated. But I also think it has to do with our funeral traditions. When it comes to saying farewell to our loved ones, African American families can be very extravagant.

I've known people who left instructions before they died about what they wanted to wear, and that's probably wise. There are a lot of subjects families can get upset about, but oh, Lord, try getting a beloved mama into the ground without her daughters coming to blows about what she's wearing. I've even known cases where the deceased's outfit was changed twice before the actual funeral.

First of all, we insist on an open casket if at all possible. If the body isn't visible, there *will* be gossip. And, yes, the appearance of the body is something we all pay close attention to. The deceased should look like him- or herself, but just extra well rested. Some morticians get out of control and put too much makeup on the bodies, which usually leaves family and friends shaking their heads in pity. Postmortem is no time to experiment with cosmetics. No one wants their sweet aunt Gertrude looking like some ashy Jezebel when she meets Jesus.

In the South, when someone looks particularly good, we say he or she is "casket ready." We all want to be especially attractive after death. The deceased is always buried in a sharp outfit, a Sunday-best suit or a beautiful dress with all the extras: necklace, earrings, brooch, hose, their Sunday-best shoes, and sometimes gloves with a matching hat.

When a southerner dies, we take several days to say good-bye. The minute the news starts to circulate, the first thing the friends and relatives do is start cooking, because we're going to the home of the deceased bearing the best comfort foods: pies, casseroles, cakes, pot roast, fried chicken. And if the family is known to partake in adult beverages, a bottle of the finest liquor is always welcomed and appropriate. A Southern Belle will have a signature dish—like my famous sweet potato soufflé—for occasions like this. She'll also always have a couple of discreet, reliable dark outfits in her closet that she can put on without a second thought. Your attire has to be appropriate for the family you are sitting with. You never want to appear as if you are attempting to be the center of attention at such a sensitive time.

Pearl of Wisdom

When you arrive at a house in mourning you take your dish into the kitchen. It's a courtesy to the family to tape your name and a description of what you brought to the bottom of your dish, because someone is going to write a thank-you note and hopefully return the dish. So you might as well make it easy for them.

People from my religious background don't drink, officially. Which doesn't mean that nobody ever drinks or gets drunk. It just means they don't do it openly in a setting like this. But there is always someone with a glass of punch that seems to have an extra kick to it or a Styrofoam cup with a beverage that looks like sweet tea but smells like a New York alley. While everybody knows what is really going on, no one ever questions it. However, no respectable lady is ever caught dead drinking during the "sitting." It is usually the men who partake. And this is true for all of the events surrounding the funeral.

Before the funeral, there is always a viewing or a wake. There's a lot of variety in the format, depending on what the family wants and the facilities of the funeral home they're working with. But normally the viewing is a day or two before the funeral. The body is presented to the family for approval before any public viewing takes place. Upon the family's approval the body—looking as beautiful as possible—is presented to the public. All of the flower arrangements are prominently placed around the casket with the cards of the people who sent them attached. For southern folks, the number and extravagance of the floral arrangements directly correlate with the person's standing in the community. In the African American community, the funeral director and funeral home are held in high esteem, so people always come appropriately dressed whether they are making arrangements or viewing a body. Because culturally, African Americans are very emotional, it is not strange to see people kissing the body and holding the hands of the deceased, wailing and weeping, and sometimes even attempting to crawl into the casket. Emotions can run extremely high and the most normally serene person can transform into a weeping basket case at the site of their late loved one.

We are demonstrative down South. It's a matter of honor, respect, and a way of showing how much we loved the deceased. It would be a disgrace to have a funeral or a wake where nobody cried. But of course it can go overboard. You see people genuinely fainting, while others pretend to faint for attention. When I direct a funeral, I make sure to have mounds of tissue to gently dab away tears and handheld fans to provide my mourners with fresh air. I do my best to assist in the event of a sudden collapse or fainting spell, but being a petite princess I am not always the sturdiest pillar to lean on.

During the wake you get everyone to sit down and there's a little more structure. The pastor leads everyone in a prayer, and maybe there's a reading and possibly a few hymns and a solo. Then the mourners can take turns to speak. Usually the family members will lead off, but after that anyone who wants to can step up to the microphone and tell a story or make a comment. If they start to run on too long, the pastor will step in and gently hustle them away from the microphone or say something like, "Thank you, brother, for your heartfelt contribution." That's usually when someone collapses in tears and can't say another word.

The funeral is the climax of the whole sequence of events. It's the most public and the most formal part of saying farewell. Most people wear traditional black church attire, and Southern Belles will have a special funeral hat that they save for these occasions, whether it's a fierce fascinator or a big-brimmed hat with a veil or a bow. The outfit's finished with dark stockings, refined jewelry, and a small black pocketbook that's just big enough to hold your car keys and a handker-chief. We expect to express grief, so you will need tissue as a backup. And this is definitely a time for a waterproof mas-cara. (Go ahead and test it first in the shower; the Belle is all about research.)

Family—and we define this term pretty broadly—sits up front, of course. This makes them highly visible. Naturally there are family members who live for the drama of being in the family procession. To walk down the aisle alongside the family as a member or a participant in the service is note-worthy. Most funerals include a section of tributes from fam-ily and friends. Sometimes it's comparable to a concert, with musical selections performed by the best singers and musi-cians in town. The Southern Belle is perfectly happy to speak or sing if her contribution is requested, but she'll never hog the microphone.

Normally the burial comes next, so we all troop out of the church and into the latest models of limousines and cars and drive in a procession to the cemetery. (We don't usually cre-mate in the South; we figure if we wanted to burn we'd just live recklessly and go to hell.) Since the funeral is the most public and well attended of the last rites, being assigned to ride in the car following the limousine confirms to everyone that you are closest to the deceased, which gives you funeral "celebrity" status for the day. Naturally that should be the immediate family, but sometimes family structure in the South is pretty complicated and doesn't correlate with actual blood relations. It's not unusual to hear people call a close family friend an aunt, uncle, or cousin. While there might be absolutely no DNA connection, if that "aunt" or "uncle" is not listed on the program with the other relatives, I assure you there will be problems after or possibly during the service.

The graveside ceremony can be the opportunity for a lot of special little touches. Even if the family doesn't opt for a horse-drawn carriage for the casket or the musical hearse (music for the benefit of everyone around, not for the deceased, of course), they might have doves, a balloon release, a trumpeter, a second line, or simply the opportunity to place roses on the casket before interment. I love all these formalities and I truly believe they can make people feel better. We all need a little ritual to get us through the tough times.

We also need to eat and celebrate, and no event as significant as a funeral could ever occur without feasting and merriment following it. The repast is as important as the funeral service. Depending on the family, the repast can be held at the church's reception hall or in a fine restaurant or banquet hall, but the main objective is to celebrate and end the day with decadent dishes. Again, the family of mourners is special: they sit together and are served first along with the funeral director. No one would dare touch a roll before the family is seated and the food is blessed. It's a lavish meal full of southern delicacies, with lots of opportunity for fellowship and sharing. Things sometimes get a little jolly with the aid of liquor, but of course the Southern Belle wouldn't know anything about that.

You may be reading this and wondering how long it takes us to bury our dead down South. The answer is—pretty much all day. Count on at least two hours in the church. The graveside ceremony alone could take half an hour, and most cemeteries are on the outskirts of town. So with the driving time, then the repast afterward, the day is more or less gone. But spending a day in tribute to a friend or family member seems perfectly sensible to southerners. And besides, hopefully someday people will do it for you.

° Recipes °

You didn't think I was going to talk about our wonderful Southern cuisine without giving you a few recipes, did you?

PHAEDRA'S SOUTHERN BELLE SWEET TEA

There's always a pitcher of this tea in a Belle's refrigerator, and we often drink it with meals. Not to be confused with the hot drink the English are so crazy about! Sweet tea is a staple beverage in the South; with the warm, humid climate, sweat tea is an instant referesher.

Ingredients

3 cups water

1 family-size black tea bag or 3 regular-size black tea bags

1 cup sugar or to taste

1 cup tepid water (room temperature)

½ cup Country Time presweetened lemonade mix

Fresh lemon slices, mint, peaches, or strawberries for garnish

Instructions

1. In a medium pot, bring 3 cups of water to a boil. Turn off the pot and add tea bags. Allow tea to steep for 10 minutes. Remove tea bags.

2. In a large pitcher, add warm tea, sugar, and lemonade mix, stirring until sugar and lemonade mix is completely dissolved. Add tepid water and an additional 4 cups of water and stir until well mixed. Chill and serve in tall glasses over ice cubes. Garnish with fresh lemon, mint, peaches, or strawberries.

NOTE: Sweetness can be personalized by adding more water or ice to the tea.

NOTE: To give your tea a specific fruit flavor, add fruit puree or nectar to tea while tea is warm. Add more water to dilute if the tea becomes too thick.

SOUTHERN BISCUITS

This recipe calls for self-rising flour, which we Belles often use for baking. It's got the baking powder and some salt already included.

Ingredients

2¼ cups self-rising flour, plus extra for dusting

1 tablespoon sugar

¾ cup shortening

1 cup buttermilk (or whole milk)

1 tablespoon melted butter

Instructions

1. Preheat oven to 425 degrees.

2. In a large bowl, mix the flour and sugar. Using a pastry cutter or a pair of butter knives, cut the shortening into the mix until it resembles coarse meal. Gradually add the buttermilk, blending the dough by hand. When the dough begins to pull away from the sides of the bowl, it is ready to cut into biscuits.

3. Pat and roll out dough on a nonstick surface or cut a brown paper bag in half and dust with flour. Thickness of the rolled-out dough should be 1 to 1½ inches. Cut biscuits with a large juice glass dipped in flour or use a biscuit cutter. Repeat until all dough is used. Place on a lightly greased baking sheet.

4. Bake for 20 to 25 minutes or until golden brown.

5. Upon removal from oven, brush biscuit tops with butter.

Don't overhandle the dough. Too much handling will make your biscuits tough.

THE BELLE'S BEST MACARONI AND CHEESE

You may think you know how to make macaroni and cheese—but this is the Belle's version!

Ingredients

8 ounces elbow macaroni
2 eggs

¾ cup whole milk

½ cup half-and-half

½ cup heavy cream

½ teaspoon chopped parsley

¼ teaspoon sugar

Pinch cayenne pepper

¾ teaspoon sea salt

½ tablespoon ranch seasoning

10 ounces sharp cheddar cheese, grated

5 ounces Havarti cheese, grated

5 ounces Parmesan cheese, grated

5 ounces of Fontina cheese, grated

Instructions

1. Preheat the oven to 350 degrees.

2. Cook the macaroni according to package directions, drain, and set aside.

3. In a large mixing bowl, beat the eggs. Add the milk, half-and-half, cream, parsley, sugar, cayenne, salt, and ranch seasoning and mix until well blended.

4. Add the macaroni and the cheddar, Havarti, Parmesan, and Fontina cheeses, and mix until fully incorporated. Leave a handful of cheddar aside for garnish.

5. Pour into a large baking dish and garnish top with grated cheddar cheese. Cover dish with aluminum foil and bake for 30 to 35 minutes.

6. Remove the foil and leave the dish in the oven long enough for the cheese to melt.

Pearl of Wisdom

Here's a perfect Southern Belle trick: perfect because it just requires a little bit of advance planning, but has big impact. When you're entertaining in warm weather, you can elevate absolutely any kind of cool drink by making fancy ice cubes. Float a little lemon curl or an edible flower in the ice trays. Or freeze juice to drop into iced tea. You can even buy ice trays with great shapes like stars and flowers; freeze batches in advance and store them in the freezer in Tupperware—next to that batch of cheese straws that you keep there for unexpected company.

What's That?—Pimiento Cheese

It's pretty shocking to a southerner to be told that pimiento cheese is a local specialty, because to us it is completely ordinary. Frankly, I don't know how you live without it in other parts of the country. It's such a basic that you could easily end up eating it three or four times a week, on Ritz crackers, stuffed into celery, on white bread, toasted, grilled, melted onto a hot dog or hamburger, and in salads or baked potatoes.

The three basic ingredients are sharp cheddar cheese, chopped pimientos, and mayonnaise. People add all kinds of other ingredients to dress it up, like garlic or hot red pepper, or sometimes Monterey Jack cheese to smooth out the flavor a little. The one thing you must do if you make pimiento cheese sandwiches is cut the crusts off. That's what makes them civilized.

The Belle-O-Meter Quiz

So, ladies, how are you doing? I'm sure you've all been very attentive to my suggestions and are amazed by the results. You're probably totally used to a steady diet of compliments and flirtation and invitations. But here's a little quiz in case you feel the need to measure how far you've come.

1. Your routine greeting when you meet a new person is:
   a) A surly glare.
   b) "Hi."
   c) "Well, hello! How are you today?"

2. If you're trying on a dress at a shop that doesn't have a three-way mirror, you:
   a) Go ahead and buy it and hope it looks all right from the back.
   b) Ask the saleswoman nicely if there's a better mirror in another dressing room.
   c) Ask the saleswoman nicely if she would photograph

you from behind with your phone so you can see the
results for yourself.

3. You have new friends coming for dinner. The thermo-
stat in your oven is broken, and the cake you baked is
still raw in the middle. You:
a) Just don't serve dessert.
b) Slice up some fruit and hope for the best.
c) Cut off the cooked bits of cake. Whip up a custard
sauce. Pour it over the cake fragments, dust the whole
thing with cocoa powder, and serve the portions in
champagne glasses.

4. Your best friend is dating a man you don't trust. You:
a) Tell her exactly that.
b) Get some dirt on him and share it with her.
c) Take her to brunch and get her to tell you what she
likes so much about him. After all, maybe you're wrong.

5. If your gentleman friend brought you a corsage to wear
on a date you would:
a) Put it in the refrigerator. Nobody wears corsages
nowadays!
b) Pin it to your coat collar and check your coat.
c) Pin it in an unusual spot like your waist or behind
your ear, after extracting one little blossom to put in
his lapel.

6. Your favorite heel height is:
   a) Flat.
   b) From one and a half to two inches, ladylike but comfortable.
   c) Nothing under three inches, except at the gym.

7. You hear that a so-called friend has been gossiping about you. Your reaction is to:
   a) Confront her.
   b) Spread rumors about her.
   c) Behave extra sweetly to her.

8. You are traveling in a small plane and told that you must lighten your baggage. You decide to leave behind:
   a) Your hair dryer.
   b) Your straightening iron.
   c) Your spare hair dryer.

Of course you don't need a key—you know that if your answers are mostly "a" it's time to go back and read this little book again. If they are mostly "b" you are well on your way, and if mostly "c," you are a genuine Southern Belle. So maybe it's time to share your new skills with a friend and pass along this book. I hope it's been helpful to you.

With my very best wishes,

Phaedra

° *Acknowledgments* °

Every Southern Belle is aware of the fact that knowing how and when to say "please" and "thank you" are hallmarks of true charm, grace, and hospitality—so please indulge me while I take this opportunity to express my sincerest gratitude to all of the people who helped me take this book from dream to reality. It has been an amazing journey and I thank God, first and foremost, for the traveling mercies and ever-present providence.

My grandmother, Hazel Meadows and aunt, Frances Meadows, both of beloved memory, were the ultimate Southern Belles who shared with me their wisdom and wit. I would also like to honor the memory of Angela "Nena" Thomas, a dear friend and sister of my spirit, who was taken from us far too soon. I will be forever grateful to have had these women in my life. I miss each of you. You may be gone from this world, but you remain in my heart and thoughts.

My brother, Henri Jacques Parks, has been a steady rock even during the most turbulent of times. Your constant encouragement and the reliability of your presence have made all the difference; thank you.

I also want to thank my other siblings, Albert and Keosha Bell, for always offering a hand and for being there through thick and thin.

Thank you, again and again, to my mom for everything.

Southern families tend to come in two sizes: big and bigger. The names of all the members of my extended family are too numerous to mention here, but I would like them to know that I am grateful to each and every one of them for filling my life with good times, good food, and good wishes, and for always holding me firmly in their embrace.

When it comes to family, I have been twice blessed to be equally sustained by the compassion and commitment of individuals to whom I am eternally bound, entirely by choice and desire.

I can't remember a time when my friends Kandi Burruss, Melanie Comeaux Drake, Nabs and Audra Fowler, Venita Kite James, Schanea Fleming Kelly, Kenyette Miller, Angela Robinson Thomas, and Monique "Whyte Chocolate" Williams were not in my life. Together we have traveled hills and valleys. Thank you for walking beside me and for being such wonderful company.

I would also like to thank my prayer sisters, LaTonia Hines, Adriene Nettles Huddlestun, Corriya Burns, Toni Griffin, and LaToya Cooper for always having my back. The greatest pleasure of our friendship is its foundation in faith, which has kept us grounded through the years, and enabled us to urge each other forward.

There have been several fine Southern Gentlemen who have graced my life with their charm, chivalry, wit, intelligence, and loyalty: Ted "Touche" Lucas; and, my confidant and advisor, Mayor M. Kasim Reed. You guys are simply the best.

My friend Meri Nana-Ama Danquah always believed that I should and would do a book. I thank her for guiding me through this process and, despite the initial obstacles and challenges, for persevering with me while I found my footing on this literary terrain.

It was my good fortune to find myself, and this project, in the care of Emma Sweeney, my agent. Thank you for recognizing my vision, and for showing such great enthusiasm.

Thank you to everyone at Gallery Books for giving this book a special place in your house, and for all the time and hard work that was invested in every single page and element of it. I am especially grateful to Jennifer Bergstrom, the vice president and publisher; Louise Burke, the president; Stephanie DeLuca in publicity; and my editor, Emilia Pisani.

Many, many thank-yous to Carol Wallace, wordsmith extraordinaire. Certainly this book would not have become what it is without your dedication and talent.

To my staff, especially Stephen Wang, I appreciate your loyalty and commitment to excellence.

The power of love is nothing short of miraculous. It tests, it teaches, and it transforms. I am reminded of this every single day with my husband, Apollo Nida, and our two sons. This life that we are making and sharing is a source of strength for all I do. None of this would have been possible without you, the ones who matter most. Thank you.